CONVERSATIONS *with* MARY

CONVERSATIONS

with

MARY

*Messages of Love, Healing,
Hope, and Unity for Everyone*

ANNA RAIMONDI

ATRIA BOOKS

NEW YORK   LONDON   TORONTO   SYDNEY   NEW DELHI

ATRIA
B O O K S

An Imprint of Simon & Schuster, Inc.
1230 Avenue of the Americas
New York, NY 10020

First Atria Books hardcover edition October 2017

ATRIA B O O K S and colophon are trademarks of Simon & Schuster, Inc.

For information about special discounts for bulk purchases, please contact Simon & Schuster Special Sales at 1-866-506-1949 or business@simonandschuster.com.

The Simon & Schuster Speakers Bureau can bring authors to your live event. For more information, or to book an event, contact the Simon & Schuster Speakers Bureau at 1-866-248-3049 or visit our website at www.simonspeakers.com.

Interior design by Suet Chong
Floral pattern by Nataliia Litovchenko / Shutterstock, Inc.

Manufactured in the United States of America

10 9 8 7 6 5 4 3 2 1

Library of Congress Cataloging-in-Publication Data is available.

ISBN 978-1-5011-5635-9
ISBN 978-1-5011-5637-3 (ebook)

This book is dedicated to you, the reader,
and to people everywhere who seek a connection
with God, Allah, Jehovah, or the power of the universe.
I pray that this book opens your mind and heart
as it awakens your soul. I hope you permit Mary's
healing energy and enduring love to guide you on
your journey through life.

May you be able to open your ears and heart

to me, the Mother, as I guide you

and lead you to peace.

CONTENTS

A NOTE TO THE READER

This book, at its heart, is a conversation. Conversations develop, wander, deepen, and, when they are good, they inspire new dialogue. On these pages you will have the opportunity to read Mary's messages to us all, as she wrote this book through me. While these chapters are based in theme, Mary has her own ideas on how this conversation should go and what she'd like to talk about! As such, subjects may overlap or stray from the initial chapter theme but it is my hope (and hers for that matter) that this conversation rise and fall a bit like a wave, carrying you, the reader, from one piece of wisdom to the next.

It should also be noted that God, as referred to in this book, is a God for all people. God doesn't belong to one group and not to another. He loves us all. You will learn from reading these pages that Mary, in her conversations, doesn't discriminate between or among religions and religious teachings. God is a power above all, the Creator of the universe, and a perfect energy of Love. God does not have a gender, but "he" is used in this book for the sake of simplicity. Please remember that Mary is for all people. She repeats this over and over; we are all her children regardless of our religion or spiritual belief. She is the universal mother of humanity. Her mantle is wide and she wants all people to seek sanctuary under it. Also, make no mistake: *You did not choose this book to read; Mary chose it for you because you need it.*

I have been instructed by Mary to put specific meditations at the end of each chapter. It is her hope that you will perform these meditations after reading the chapters. The goal here is to enable you, the reader, to enter a state of grace and be able to take in her words not only with your mind, but also with your heart and soul. On the following pages are some guidelines for getting the most out of your meditations. It is my belief that, with devotion and focus, you may hear Mary and/or feel her, as I do. May God bless you and be with you as you awaken spiritually through the meditations set forth on these pages as well as through messages that Mary brings to you.

SUGGESTIONS WHILE MEDITATING

+ If you have never meditated before, you may require some practice in shutting down your mind and just permitting yourself "to be." I think you'll find that the more you meditate, the easier it becomes to connect to the energy of God and all in the Divine realm.

+ Allow yourself to meditate at a time when you know you will not be disturbed. Shut off all electronic devices such as phones, televisions, computers, etc. Find a quiet place. It is best to sit with your back supported instead of lying down so that you stay awake.

+ Keep your expectations simple and let the meditation be what it is. There is no need to overthink.

+ When you meditate your goal should be to stay present in the moment, not focused on the past or the future. It is a form of surrendering and opening up to your soul and all that you are to God (our egos don't like this as it is a place of "no thought" and lack of control).

+ Note that many people experience "monkey chatter" or a nonending stream of thoughts as they attempt to meditate. This is very common. I like to think of it as your ego screaming for you to remain in control and focus on the day-to-day problems and issues instead of being present in the moment. Just image these thoughts floating away from you with the silent promise you will return to them at a later time.

+ Part of meditation is the act of focusing on one's breath. Many people have discovered that breath work allows them to remain in the present. If you find focused breathing useful, aim to breathe in through the nose and out through either the mouth or the nose, whichever feels most comfortable.

+ Try not to let worry or stress enter your body.

+ Consider putting forth an intention or say a prayer in your mind before actually meditating. The intention can be as simple as "help me to open my heart," or you may have something more specific to your personal needs or those of your family.

+ Although I like to meditate in silence, many people like to play some peaceful meditation music. Feel free to experiment and find the best way for you to achieve a wonderful meditative experience.

+ Feel free to record the text set forth in each chapter and play it back when you meditate, or you may prefer reading it first and then orchestrating the imagery in your imagination.

+ Have faith that heaven will help you get to that place and connect to your soul and God. Offer yourself to all in the heavenly realm so that they may show you the way.

+ Ask God to protect you and guide you as you connect with your soul.

CONVERSATIONS *with* MARY

PREFACE

There were two distinct events in my life that pulled me to Mary. The first took place when I was five years old. I can still feel the golden warmth of that spring afternoon. Crimson roses and dainty pink blossoms climbed up and through a small wooden whitewashed garden fence. I was alone in the backyard of the house I shared with my family in suburban Long Island. It was an average residential yard with verdant lush grass, a sturdy apple tree growing in the center, and a swing set built by my father, painted in red and white candy stripes on the right side of the lawn. There was also a small grotto in front of the apple tree where, at one time, stood a statue of Mary. The statue was long gone; probably broken and never replaced. I remember wearing an olive green and white polka dot minidress that my mother had made for me. Like any child on those first warm spring days, I was so happy to be out of the constrictive clothing of winter. As I sometimes did, that afternoon I slid my body easily into the space where the statue once was. I just sat and marveled at the day. I was that kind of a child. My eyes were wide and always absorbing the world around me. I was able to feel nature; the wonders of it all. The fresh clean smell of the dense grass was almost tangible to me. The soft breeze heightened my senses and woke me up to all that was surrounding me—both seen and unseen. I heard the gentle hum of the vacuum cleaner as my mother moved it around our small house; the stereo belted the voice of Vikki Carr singing "It Must Be Him."

Then, as I sat in the grotto, a feeling of pure and unadulterated peace overtook my body. I felt giddy with excitement although I had no frame of reference as to the reason. Every one of my senses became more attuned. I felt the cool stone beneath my little hands; its hard smooth surface under my thighs and buttocks. I smelled the sweet aroma of lilacs that graced the perimeter of the yard. I didn't dare move for fear this state of being would pass. I heard sparrows above my head shifting on the branches of the apple tree behind me and took notice as they sang their morning songs to the world. And then, among this symphony of sound, I heard her voice. It was gentle, yet strong. She said, "Anna, I am here for you always. Always come to me." A total unconditional love overtook me; there was a feeling that was and remains so extraordinary and so difficult to describe in words. People always say this—I know—but it is very true: Our language is too limited to convey spiritual feelings or to describe the wondrous feeling of Mary's presence.

I couldn't move. I didn't want to move for fear that this sensation would leave. And then suddenly, there she was, directly in front of me. Mary was smiling at me; her hands reached for me. I didn't reach out; I was stunned. I felt paralyzed. I knew without a doubt that this was Mary, although she didn't look like the renderings I had seen of her in books or even in churches. She was dressed in a well-worn brown robe; the fabric appeared rough, but radiated warmth. There was a light brown dress underneath. She had olive skin, wide, soft mahogany-colored eyes and coffee colored hair that hung to her waist where a hemp belt was tied and held her dress together. She wore a tan colored covering adorning the top of her head, but no hood. Her face stood out in repose. Her penetrating eyes captured my attention and communicated with me in a way that I can only describe as speaking to my heart. I didn't just hear her words; they became mingled with my very essence—my soul. I didn't want this rapture to end. I remember just sitting there for what seemed like hours, catatonic, as I basked in the overwhelming love of this beautiful vision. Later, I would tell my playmates of the Lady in the grotto and we would make a game of talking to her and asking her to make our dreams come true. We were children and open to all of the miracles that God put before us. The feeling of that first time still lingers and makes my heart skip a beat. And that, I believe, is what perfect love does to us all. I know what real love is. Mary showed me.

I sat for a while in the grotto. It was as though she had swaddled me in a cozy blanket of warm love. When I finally reentered the house, the sun was still kissing the mimosa tree by the back door, its pink flowers rising up to embrace the warmth of the rays. Everything seemed quieter; the birds chirped softly. The music that was coming from the house was muted; Vikki Carr was replaced by the mellifluous crooning of Dean Martin. I climbed the steps to the back door and saw my mother directly in front of me, seated at our dark brown kitchen table. She was drinking a cup of coffee and slowly inhaling a cigarette. My mother was young then, around twenty-six. I remember she wore white pedal pushers. The house smelled of Pledge and bleach and the pungent aroma of coffee; a haze of cigarette smoke lingered and left a stale peppery odor.

I walked over to the chair opposite her and sat down, my feet dangling. I asked her if she had ever seen or spoken to Mary. Without looking up she took a drag off her cigarette and turned a page in her magazine. "Mary who?" she asked.

"Mary, the lady in church," I gingerly answered.

My mother lifted her head. Her eyes met mine. A long silence passed before she rested her cigarette in the ashtray and told me, as matter-of-factly as she could, that she wanted to know what this was all about. And so I told her what I had seen, that Mary had talked to me. She wasn't nearly as shocked or dismissive as I would imagine another adult might be. You must understand that my mother was a believer long before me. Both my parents were deeply religious. She gently expressed that she believed some people were truly gifted and that if I saw Mary, then I should continue to pray and believe. My confession turned out to be a joyous occasion for my family. When my father learned of our conversation, he mirrored my mother's sentiments.

In retrospect, I realize that this was the perfect way for Mary to introduce herself to me and at the most ideal time in my life. I was simply a child, not yet marred by convention or the judgment of others. I led with my heart and was in tune with my soul. I felt the power of God in nature but was too young to give voice to it. Mary alleviated all my fear and her love washed over me and held me still. There was something about her beauty, serenity, and love that filled me with immediate faith. In my innocence, I had no reason to question why she was coming to me or how this was possible. All I can say is that the experience was profound.

While I now hear her and sense her in all that I do, I have never actually seen her in that way again. I try not to question why and I understand now, after years of hoping to see her again, that I don't really need to see her with my eyes. Feeling her presence around me and within me, really connecting to her essence, is far more important. What she looks like doesn't matter; it is what she says and how she makes me feel that is far more significant.

Decades later, on a bitter freezing day in the winter of 1989, I left the building where I worked, bundled in a puffy coat zipped up to my chin, my eyes peering out from a tight ski hat. It was the lunch hour. I was in my late twenties and felt as though my life was going nowhere. I was married and yearned to have a child, yet couldn't conceive; my job was not fulfilling and I felt that I was just robotically going through the motions of life without passion. I was disillusioned with life and becoming depressed. At the time, I was working on Madison Avenue. I detested my job and it added to my feelings of being lost and empty. I felt stuck on a path that I didn't want to be traveling on. In fact, I felt as though someone had put their grimy hand into a crevice of my chest and yanked out my slow beating heart. I was becoming part of the "rat race" and was, on an emotional and soul level, rebelling. The business world was more than I could handle. It was aggressive and uncaring. None of it was working for me.

As I turned to walk, the wind viciously slapped my cheeks, bringing tears to my eyes. Madison Avenue was crowded with people walking briskly, everyone rushing from one place to another, everyone with a purpose. I felt as if I was pushing and shoving my way down the street. This was my life. I felt achy, uncomfortable physically and emotionally. I didn't know where to go to feel alive again. And then, in that maze of people, between the blare of a siren, the heavy wail of a city bus, and the tap of a spatula from a nearby food cart, I heard a gentle whisper; I felt a calming presence—it told me to go to Mary. I didn't pause to think, my feet seemed to move of their own volition and I headed south to St. Patrick's Cathedral.

As I entered the cathedral the pungent aroma of incense welcomed me. The flickering orange and yellow glow of candles lit the darkened church as people milled around, some praying and some just taking in the magnificence of the structure itself. I headed back to the Lady Chapel. As I approached the small sanctuary, I dug into my purse for change to light a candle. The quiet was almost surreal compared to the blaring city that was just outside. I flinched as the coins rattled when I dropped them into the tin collection box. Their sound resonated. I lit a small pearl-colored prayer candle on the top row of the black metal rickety stand. Then I stood, gazing. The flame quivered initially but soon grew, boldly licking the air around it. The thought struck me: was I stuck in a weak moment in my life? I felt very insubstantial and hollow. I couldn't even conjure an intention or prayer as I lit that candle. The lighting in the chapel was dazzling and the prominent statue of Mary loomed above the dozen or so hazel colored, worn wooden pews in front of it. I found an unoccupied spot in the back, kneeled, and let the tears flow unabashedly. As I fervently began to pray the Rosary, using my fingers instead of saying the prayers on the beads, a tranquillity came over me. I felt as though the raging tornado in my heart had been settled. The teardrops ceased and I heard Mary. She said that it was all fine; that she had brought my prayers to God and they were answered. She gave me hope; I believed her and at that moment I knew it was all going to be okay. I felt like someone was breathing peace into my soul. I raised my eyes to the statue of Mary in front of me as my heart fluttered with gratitude. My face was streaked with the remnants of my tears, and what I saw took my breath away. A baby boy, wrapped in a shimmery ivory colored blanket was nestled in the arms of the statue of Mary. I was transfixed. My heart began to drum wildly in my chest. The experience was exhilarating. Mary instructed me to look into the luminous brown eyes of this baby. And then she said, "When he comes to you, you will recognize him by his eyes. And you will feel the blessings of God." In September 1990 my son was born. I remember gazing into his warm brown eyes and truly knowing that God was blessing my family.

Twenty-six years later, in the autumn of 2015, Mary came to me as I sat outside my house in Connecticut in the early evening. I had just returned from Medjugorje (pronounced Meh-jah-gor-ee-ah) a region in Bosnia and Herzegovina known for being the location where Mary appeared to six local children in 1981. These children described Mary as a woman wearing a white gown and a crown with twelve stars on her head and holding a baby in her arms. Mary appeared to the children many times and is still appearing monthly to one of them, Mirjana Dragicevic, who continues to live in Medjugorje. Pilgrims from all over the world still flock to this little rural town to be in the energy of Mary.

Now back home, I relaxed on a worn teak chair, my feet snug in my slippers, propped comfortably on the gray stone wall at the edge of the deck, and thought about the trip. I realized that I didn't feel any closer to Mary than I had prior to the journey. It suddenly dawned on me that I didn't need to go across the world to find her because she has always been with me. This realization seemed to calm me and bring me peace.

The peepers croaked in the woods and, on occasion, there came the sound of a scurrying animal or the shadow of a bird flying from branch to branch. I tilted my head back and looked up at the sky. I was taken with the vastness of it. The stars glittered and I remember feeling so minuscule, so insignificant in the immensity of it all. I felt my heart, a vigorous beat in my chest, as the sky enveloped me. I gazed up at the sky for what seemed like hours but was probably only minutes. Then, I began to feel Mary . . . she floated into my senses and I welcomed her. Mary softly, yet emphatically, told me that she was the mother of humanity and she desired to use me as her channel to bring her messages to multitudes of people of all religions, ethnicities, and races. She said the time was upon us to learn how to be closer to God and to find joy and peace in our lives.

Although she was gentle, there was an urgency about her. I felt a sensation of panic. Mary calmed my fears and told me that she would speak through me so that the world could be saved. She told me that there would be more and more people who would hear her through me and who would be drawn to the Divine light. Mary assured me that she would bring the right people to me. And so it came to be within a short period of time. Various paths and introductions led me to the vehicle Mary wished to use—this book that you hold in your hands. Two years ago I had not a single thought in my head of writing a book yet shortly after that night I had a book deal with one of the preeminent book publishers in the world. Before long, the first words of this book were being typed onto my computer screen, from Mary through me. This is the way she wanted the world to hear her and I am so honored to be the one she chose to bring her words forward. And I know, without doubt, that this is only the beginning.

INTRODUCTION

I have always felt a profound duty to share with others the Mary that I had come to know over the years. This eventually led to large seminars, retreats, and classes that taught people how to connect to Mary, feel her presence, and hear her voice. When I communicate with her, she most often "appears" as a feeling of overwhelming, unconditional, and nurturing love. I also clearly hear her strong yet loving voice. It is in this way that I understand what she wants to convey to me. Mary has chosen to come to me in this manner. She is as real to me as any material person could ever be. A peacefulness overcomes my body as my thoughts are immediately pushed aside and a sense of pure euphoria and rapture envelopes me. It is a feeling that defies explanation. It is as complicated as defining love . . . because that is truly what it is. God *is* love.

Mary is love just as God is love and just as we are all created in the image of love. Mary has led me and traveled with me on this life's journey to bring forward her healing and her love for ALL people. She doesn't speak to me of division in religions or ethnicities, rather she speaks of unity and the oneness of humanity. Mary does not dictate the way it should be, but rather the way it can be to reach peace and love and, most importantly, to unite with God through our hearts and souls. Mary tells me the way it could be, if we open our eyes and awaken to the Truth that applies to all.

Although people often associate Mary with Roman Catholicism, she does not belong to just one religion or one group of people. Mary is so much more than this. In fact, to truly appreciate the conversations that this book encompasses it is important for you, the reader, to have a clear understanding of who Mother Mary is on a global level.

Mary is known to many different religions and societies. She has been called many different names, like Quan Yin and Maria Kannon, depending on the religion or culture. Mary is revered by Christians and Muslims as the holy mother of Jesus; in fact, she is mentioned more times in the Quran than in the New Testament. She is also admired by Jews and others as a figure of feminine strength and courage.

According to the Quran, Mary, "a saintly woman" (*siddigah*) was destined, together with Jesus, her son, to be "a sign (*ayah*) to the universe" (Quran The Prophets XXI:91), to play a unique role in the history of salvation. Mary is mentioned frequently in the Quran and a majority of Muslims view her as one of the most righteous women to have ever lived. Muslim tradition, like Christian, honors her memory at Matariyyah near Cairo, and in Jerusalem. Muslims also visit the Bath of Mary in Jerusalem, where Muslim tradition recounts Mary once bathed, and this location is visited at times by women who are seeking a cure for barrenness. The birth of Mary is narrated in the Quran with references to her father as well as her mother. Mary's father is called Amran (Imran in Arabic) in tradition and is the equivalent of Joachim in Christian tradition. Her mother is called Anne (Hannah in Arabic), which is the same name as in Christian tradition (Saint Anne). Muslim literature narrates that Amran and his wife were old and childless and that, one day, the sight of a bird in a tree feeding her young aroused Anne's desire for a child. She prayed to God to fulfill her desire and vowed, if her prayer was accepted, that her child would be dedicated to the service of God.

Jews respect Mary as a Jewish woman of lineage, strength, and character. She grew up in a Jewish home, practiced Jewish religious traditions, and, according to some scholars, is from the house and lineage of David. Her famous Magnificat (Luke 1:46–55) bears a close resemblance to Hannah's prayer of praise in 1 Samuel 2 of the Old Testament.

The Mahayana Buddhists adore Maria Kannon, also known as Quan Yin, who, similar to Mother Mary in Christian traditions, embodies the love and compassion of the mother. Even today, Kannon is widely worshipped by Buddhists in Japan and Asia. Like Mother Mary, Kannon is an expression of the feminine aspect of the Divine, a personification of love and compassion, a savior in calamity, and a miracle worker. She appears to her devotees as a lovely, gentle lady of heavenly beauty, sometimes exuding the scent of sweet flowers (in Christian tradition she makes herself known by bringing through with her the fragrance of roses). In China, she is known as Quan Yin (One Who Hears the Prayers of the World).

Much like the Virgin Mary, the Chinese Quan Yin/Maria Kannon is said to have lived a human life of extreme self-sacrifice and holiness before she ascended into heaven and became a celestial Goddess of Mercy and Compassion. Since her ascension she has been appearing as "a woman in white" to those in need of help. Her devotees respond to her loving care by honoring her on her birthday and coming in pilgrimage to her holy places on mountains, in caves, and in temples. There have been apparitions of her at P'u-t'o Sha in the Cave of Tidal Sounds, where a brilliant light miraculously shone on them, and Quan Yin appeared, sitting on a rock above the cave. This is similar to Mary's appearances in Fatima and other places around the world.

Our Lady of Guadalupe is one of the most reproduced female likenesses ever. Mary's image has even made its way to designer jewelry which is sold in large department stores and small boutiques across the globe. *National Geographic* magazine recently published a feature about Mary that went viral. Mark Burnett and Roma Downey produced two successful miniseries, *The Bible* and *A.D. The Bible Continues*, where Mother Mary is portrayed as a particularly fascinating, multilayered woman.

Mary's messages are global, forward-thinking, and transformative. When I asked her why she desires to become even more relevant to both Christians and non-Christians, she told me that her time is now, and that people around the world are finally listening. We are crying for help, she says, we are desiring a deeper sense of how heaven can alleviate our burdens. We are seeking our individual spiritual cores, an awakening, and a form of peace. Mary has told me that as a species we are finally able to accept her messages with open hearts and without fear of judgment. She maintains that there should be no boundaries between religions, ethnicities, or race. She insists that we need to see ourselves and the Creator in everyone we meet, because we are all children of God.

Among her other attributes, Mary's humility, strength, perseverance, love, and faith draw us to her, but her humanity makes her one of us. Mary isn't just a revered spiritual icon; she was a real person. Her story speaks of her "humanness": her joy, love, faith, and pain. She was a young pregnant teen who fought the social norms of her culture, had to flee as a refugee with an infant to a strange land to avoid military action (Herod ordered that all boys two years old and under be put to death in Bethlehem), struggled with political upheaval related to her son, and ultimately witnessed his torture and death. This brave and courageous woman knows what it is to feel both love and pain, and can sympathize with our anguish. As such, Mary is more relatable;

and a more familiar and accessible link to heaven. She's a tangible symbol of suffering, sacrifice, steadfast values, and unconditional feminine love. By bringing forth Jesus, the healer, the savior, the prophet, she has been crowned the mother of us all. She is with us through the labor of living in this world, helping us renew who we are spiritually.

1

Why Do You Come to Us?

How Does Mary Speak to Us and
Why Does She Speak Now?

ANNA: Mother Mary, I am so grateful, not only for myself, but also for all those who have been called to read your words in this book. Before we talk about why you're here, I want to understand who you are. There is so little written about you. Do we need to know more?

MARY: You bring me great joy by allowing me to speak to you and the world! I am bringing you and all those who are listening entry into my loving heart. Yes, what you say is true; there is very little written about me and yet I continue to speak through those who see, hear, and feel me. I have spoken through people for eons. As it is written, "Whoever has ears to hear, let them hear" (Mark 4:9). This is my prayer. I desire people not only to hear my words, but to allow my wisdom to become a part of their lives. Permit me to be your mother, your confidant, and teacher. Follow my truth so that I may lead you all to God. What little is written about me in religious texts speaks of the young woman who in strong faith followed the will of God. I was chosen and I obeyed. I lost my child to a horrible death. My journey included unbearable pain . . . yet God gave me the strength to go on. My life had merit and was important. There is no life that isn't significant. Every life touches other lives and weaves the threads that create the carpet of humanity. My life is an example of true faith and love for God. My life wasn't perfect but my love was. What's more relevant is not who I was on earth but the messages I want to bring forward now.

ANNA: What was it like for you, a woman of pure faith, to lose a child?

MARY: The agony I felt and the tears I cried are still with me. There is no greater pain. My heart weeps now for all those who must endure the pain of losing a child. Parents are bonded to their children through a love that is as close to unconditional love as can be known on earth. Even as time moved on, and I began to recognize the purpose of my son's life and death, my pain was raw. I accepted his life's journey and my part in it. Yet, I still missed the person that he was, but knew it was to be. I was a human and didn't understand it fully. My faith allowed me the wisdom to understand the purpose of Jesus's life, but didn't eliminate the horror of his death and persecution.

ANNA: I can hear the pain in your voice and feel it in your energy. That must have been very difficult for you.

MARY: It was as difficult as life on earth can ever be. I knew he lived for a bigger purpose and took my solace in that. I never lost my faith and belief in God. It was the strength that God provided for me that helped me through to the last days of my life.

ANNA: You say that who you were is not as relevant as your message. I understand, but I can't help but want to know all there is to know about you. What did you look like when you walked the earth? How can we visualize you in our minds? Do you think it is important for us to be able to paint a picture of you in our heads?

MARY: Oh, my daughter, you are so sincere in your quest to know all there is about me. It warms my heart that you and others are seeking to get closer to me in all ways possible. How I looked when I walked the earth is of little or no significance now. Yet, I will tell you because you desire to know me better. I was a human once and, as a Middle Eastern woman, my skin was dark, my eyes a deep brown, and I was small in stature. I looked no different from other women of my day in my homeland. My dark wavy hair came down to my waist and I adored the touch of my mother when she braided it. When I was a girl, I played, laughed, and cried as girls do. My life as a child was not extraordinary although my faith and love for God was always foremost. I came from the line of David. David was a small man and yet he was strong and ruled a nation. David's blood ran through my veins and I was like him and my ancestors in their faith and belief in God. I was taught God is above all and must be respected and venerated. Today—now—you can see me with your heart. By seeing me with your heart, you can feel my faith, strength of spirit, and love. It should not matter that I am light or dark skinned. The color of my eyes or my skin tone shouldn't be more important than the love I carry and am sharing with you and all who come to me. I am now in spirit. I look like what the beholder wants me to look like. If one wants me to be of fair skin and light eyes, so be it. If that image brings comfort, so be it. I am a being now of love and comfort. I have no skin color and all skin colors. I have no distinguishing features now and yet carry the beauty of all the world as I embrace your energies and raise your vibrations. I can be the same and one with all people. Don't be distracted by what your eyes see; rather see with your heart and feel. In 1 Samuel 16:7 it is written: "The Lord does not look at the things people look at. People look at the outward appearance, but the Lord looks at the heart." Be like the Lord. You carry his energy in your souls. Look into my heart; feel my heart and let it become your own heart. That is where you will see the real me—in your heart. Don't be so focused on what your eyes see. My daughter, and all of you who are receiving this message, please feel. Let your heart be open as it works in congruence with your mind. Then you will see who I am to you. That is most significant and what will be best for you and all people in moving back to the Truth.

ANNA: And so, if some people see you in different ways culturally or racially, is that all right with you?

MARY: Yes, it is right and good. The soul has no color. It is all the same. The physical body is superficial and not as beautiful as the soul. It is just a covering over the essence of the soul. I am every color and every ethnicity. I speak to all people wherever they live and whatever they look like. My image is that of the mother in whatever form that may take in your mind. However, I carry an energy that has a radiant color. Many artists over the ages have painted me with a blue dress or blue aura around me. What they saw as they connected with my energy they painted and what they painted is true. My soul vibrates a beautiful vibrant blue. Many ascribe blue as the color of royalty; so be it. I come from a royal lineage, but more important than my earthly lineage is the grace that God has bestowed upon me which vibrates as blue. Blue is the color of a high vibration. It is also the vibration of Truth. I come to you to bring you Truth. This vibration that I carry is to heal and enlighten you. I pray for the enlightenment of the world. The awakening that will bring the world to God in all his goodness.

ANNA: So you are a vibration?

MARY: My child, it is so easy to complicate that which is simple. This is only difficult to understand because it is not taught to you by your religions or in your schools. I am a soul and as a soul I am energy. The higher the energy is, the faster the vibration. "In the beginning was the Word" (John 1:1). The Word is the highest vibration as it was and is God. God is a vibration of love. As my energy vibrates it creates the color blue so that you are permitted to surround yourself with all that I am—all that I give you. I bring my vibration forward and share it to raise up all vibrations to the vibration of God—the Word incarnate, the highest vibration. Do you understand?

ANNA: I think I do . . . I have read that the principle of resonance comes when two frequencies are brought together; the lower will always rise to meet the higher. In other words, we are energy beings who carry our own unique vibration. Is that what you are saying?

MARY: Yes, that is correct! It is a purer way of comprehending the world. If you could shift out of seeing people as different, in terms of their physical attributes, and instead allow yourselves to feel their vibrations, those with the highest vibrations will be able to raise those who have the lower vibrations. I come to help the world raise its vibration.

ANNA: How can we raise our vibration and then help others?

MARY: Follow my messages . . . live in peace, compassion, and love, not just for yourselves or those in your own families and communities, but for all people. Pray for strength and courage to do so. In the world presently, those who follow this path stand out and must be brave and ready to defend the Truth. This is similar to what my son did and all the prophets who spoke of universal love, compassion, and peace. Come to me like the children you all are and allow my grace and energy to lift you up to the highest level. Take down the barriers that have been erected that separate and know that you are all energy of the light. You are all one and the same.

ANNA: We tend to separate ourselves by traits and characteristics, by "our people, our tribe." The idea that we belong to all people and on an energy level we all look like each other in an energetic sense, and like you, is comforting. Even so, I feel when you walked this earth you were so superior to us who are imperfect. You talk about David being a strong ruler, yet as written in the Old Testament, he wasn't perfect. Were you?

MARY: I know you are excited and are hanging on my every word! I desire you to share this excitement with the world. I pray that all who are reading my words will feel the excitement of the Truth building in their souls. It is right and good and why I am coming to you. What you and others need to know is that I was a flesh and bone woman; a human being like all of you and not perfect. My imperfection was born out of simply being human. Only God is perfect. Yet, I lived in surrender to God and in pure faith. It was that faith which allowed me to be more steadfast in living according to the will of God. Yet, in my imperfection, I suffered the human emotions of anger and resentment. As Jesus grew, and his mission became popular, people did not always understand him. Some thought he came to free us from the political oppression that filled my homeland while others thought he would raise us all into the place of wealth and luxury. When they didn't see the manifestation of their expectations, they mocked him and persecuted him. My own people and the Romans did this to him. I could not and did not love those that did these heinous things to my son. Jesus was my son; the child whom I brought into the world. I protected my son in word and deed when others blamed him and defiled him. I didn't always understand but I knew God had a plan and I trusted in him. I lived in reverence and in complete faith to God. I knew my life and that of my son was according to Divine will.

ANNA: It must have been very tough to surrender to the will of God as you witnessed what was being done to your son. It is something for others to strive for—to surrender amid their own suffering. You must have been very lonely in your pain. How did you handle the feeling of loneliness?

MARY: I did not love those who put my son to death until I was very old and was granted clarity from God. The friends of my son surrounded me, at the time of his death, as well as my own immediate family. They protected me and gave me comfort as I did for them. I clung to Mary from Magdala, for she so loved my son. John, the youngest, stayed by my side my entire life, loving and taking care of me. I watched as my son's friends carried out his mission. People began to follow them, seeking the Truth. This did my heart good to see that his words were being followed. And I was never alone; I had God by my side. I prayed and prayed to be in deeper union with God. But, what is more painful to a mother than the loss of her child? That is why I come to people now. I don't want to lose any of you. I want to save you from your suffering as any mother would do for her children. I want to share my wisdom with you and help you heal and save yourselves and direct you to God. Yet, like all children, you rebel and turn away. You must go through your own trials and errors. It is so painful to watch. It is time to turn to me so that I can show you peace and love. It is time to meet me so I can show you God. I am God's messenger of peace, love, and wisdom. I am here for every one of you. I desire your attention and love. I want you to know the way to save yourselves.

ANNA: You mention your parents. It is interesting that your parents are not named in the canonical Gospels, nor are they named in the Quran. But both traditions respect them as your parents. And the story of your conception and birth are very similar in both religions.

MARY: It is true that there is not much mentioned of my parents. My parents were devout in their spirituality. They prayed with great faith for my mother to conceive although she was very old. Both my parents received visitations from the angels announcing my conception. They promised God that if my mother was chosen to have a child, that the child would be given to the temple at an early age to be consecrated to God. And so it came to be. This was very difficult for them since I was their only child. With heavy hearts, yet ones filled with gratitude for their blessings, I was given to the temple at the age of three to be raised in the ways of my religion and my people. I would leave the temple upon occasion to be with my parents, whom I loved. It was with great sorrow that they passed on when I was but a young girl. They passed prior to my betrothal to Joseph well before the birth of my son.

ANNA: You have spoken to me about being a mother, but what of being a wife? Did you love Joseph, or was he just the man who completed your earthly family? Did you have other children?

MARY: I was a woman married to a man. When Joseph and I married I was but a child. Joseph was a man who had been widowed. He was wise and good and was chosen for me with great care. It was through God's initiative that he was brought to my parents for me. Because they had great faith and prayed diligently, they knew he was to be my spouse. He taught me, protected me, provided for me, and loved me. And I took care of him, loved him, and was a dutiful wife. God created man and woman to come together in love to create those in their own images. It is not sinful to create a child out of great love. By creating out of love we followed in the ways of the One who created the world out of the greatest love. With tremendous love Joseph and I had sons and daughters. Yet, Joseph passed on to heaven too soon. I mourned him as any loving wife would who loses her husband. Joseph's death left a void in my heart and in our family. By God's grace, the children were old enough to help me. I never remarried or had a need to. Many people wanted me to bring another man into my home to help me. It was unnecessary. Joseph was the one who held my heart. He was waiting for me when I entered heaven.

ANNA: I am curious about the females in your life. Did you have friends? The Bible mentions that you were close to Elizabeth. Did that relationship continue?

MARY: I had many friends as we relied upon each other in the close community where I lived. I also had daughters and female cousins who were around me. We prayed, laughed, cried, and supported each other. But Elizabeth was special to me. I loved Elizabeth and she loved me. She was many years older than me. Like my mother, she was barren and had her son late in her life. Elizabeth and I saw little of each other as the years passed. She fled with her son and husband into the desert to protect John from being murdered during the time when Herod had the firstborn males killed. She was also fearful of raising John near my son. Elizabeth was very astute. She lived longer than her husband, but she passed on while John was a young boy.

ANNA: Who then raised John?

MARY: Elizabeth was sheltered by a community of Jewish people called the Essenes. Their ways were orthodox and they lived strictly according to their interpretation of the Law. John adopted some of their ways. When he became a man, he diverted but still held much esteem for this community that took him in.

ANNA: If Jesus and John didn't grow up together how was it that they came together when they were men?

MARY: John recognized the essence and vibration of Jesus. He was not concerned with the family ties that bound them together. Rather, it was my son's energy that attracted him and bound the two together. God allowed him to see Jesus as a soul, not just as a man. And through John's "special sight," he saw all that Jesus was.

ANNA: Mother, I am so grateful for your answers. You have provided so much for me to think about. At this point, I have an understanding of who you were in life. Now, let's talk about how you come to us. I have heard and felt you my whole life, yet so many people who seek you feel they cannot hear your message, that they cannot sense your presence. You have appeared and spoken to mystics, children, and those in poor areas of the world. Why can some experience you while others can't?

MARY: My child, I love all my children. I speak to all people, yet only those who have faith and a heart that is open can hear me. I have inspired songs, poems, literature, and paintings throughout the centuries. Those who listen with their hearts can hear me. They know my voice. I am not seeking recognition; I only seek to open the door to Truth, which will bring peace for each person and the entire world. My energy is soft and subtle yet strong and persistent. I will wake people up in the middle of the night just to let them know I am praying with them. The mystics and the visionaries spread my messages in order for the world to hear. Anna, I have been speaking to you since your birth and you never denied my voice. In your innocence you sought me and I came to you and I am with you now to bring my messages to the world.

ANNA: I have felt you my whole life but why can't I see you the way the mystics have?

MARY: My dear one, all humans want to see with their eyes because there is no denying what the eyes see, or at least that is what humans think. It is more concrete than the other senses that God graced you all with. Yet, sight can be misleading. Can two people describe a rainbow in the same way? Is it any greater to see me than to feel me or hear me? I come in different ways to different people. You are all so distinct in your abilities and levels of receiving; and it is personal to each person in the world. It is the wonder of God to have created each person to be unique. The world experiences me in so many ways. To many, the apparitions are truth; to others the words are more important. I come in many ways so that my mission is complete and I am able to reach the hearts of humanity. Rejoice that others are experiencing my love and sharing it with the world! Whatever way your energy can connect with mine is good and right. Humans were graced with intelligence, yet sometimes overthinking diminishes feeling and innate knowing. You *all* know me; I am the mother. Although rational thought is good, my world is one beyond understanding, beyond the realm of rational thought. You all must recognize me by going into your hearts. It is in faith that you all will experience me; it is by opening up your hearts that you will feel me. One way of receiving is not superior to another way. I appeal to each person in a way that is perfect and right for him or her. I pray that the people of the world will allow me to touch them in whatever way is best.

ANNA: What about all those people who can't see, hear, or really feel you?

MARY: I am mother to the world; all are my children and all can connect with me. There are no elite among you; just those who have faith and an open heart. Again, I come to all who call me and allow me to embrace them. A heart of faith can unite with my energy and truly feel me. Often people don't recognize it is me coming through because they feel unworthy or it may be strange for them to believe. Or they carry fear. Fear blocks me; fear blocks God. Yet, it is me answering the questions and filling the heart and soul with the love I carry forth. All are worthy, but faith, true belief, and love allow the person to merge with my energy and experience my love in a way that is perfect and right. I implore you all, please allow me in. Let my love move you and bring you to the greatest love there is.

ANNA: Over the years you have appeared to poor people and the very young. Why is this so?

MARY: If I am called, I answer. When a heart is open to my comfort, I am there. The poor people of the world are often rich in spirit and able to yield to my words. They often live simple lives that do not have the complications that would prohibit seeing me, feeling me, and hearing me. I love children . . . they are my heart. In their innocence, they can feel my love although they may not truly know who I am. Through them, I can reach the world. And, there is no denying the words of innocent children who are speaking of things that are unknown to them. There is less reason to doubt and attribute what they are saying to anything other than to spread my words. Some people will hear and follow the words and others may need other means to hear my words and understand and follow the message. I don't come to people telling them anything that is unknown. I come to repeat words of wisdom that have been spoken by those of every religion. The way to God is through love and compassion. This is not new; it is as old as man has been walking on the earth. This concept is repeated in every God-centered religious text that has ever been written. Yet, people need to hear it again and again. And so, I come now with a power that will make people listen. Seeing me through apparitions is extraordinary and captures attention. I want your attention. I want to help you and show you how to live in peace and love as God intended you to live.

ANNA: I have often wondered if your words are somewhat translated by the receiver. You speak to so many of so many walks of life. Now, as I listen to your words, I recognize that what you say to me may not be understood and perhaps, accepted by others. Is what I am feeling true?

MARY: What you feel is true. Different people need to hear me in a way that they can understand. I am repeating the same message to all in different ways so that all can comprehend and follow my wisdom. This knowledge is beyond intelligence, it is Divine; it is what God wants you to know to bring you closer to him. Those who are reading my words here in this book can accept the way in which I come to you and then to me through you and ultimately to God. I will open their hearts to be able to accept my wisdom. Yet, they may not be open to my words as they are spoken through another person. As my vessel, I am filling you with my energy; wrapping it around your heart, mind, and soul. I am doing the same for all those who are reading my words in this book. Different messengers will attract different people, yet my message stays the same. It is still my truth. The world is large and I have many who are now helping me to do my work so that everyone in the world can align with the Truth.

ANNA: Okay, that makes sense. However, the many popular mystics who have brought you into the limelight, so to speak, have all been Catholic and their messages primarily speak to Catholics. Those messages sometimes are inconsistent with the traditions of other religions. Are you here only for the Catholics?

MARY: No, my dearest one, I come to and for all people. I have appeared to those of other religions in ways that make sense to them and their various beliefs and traditions. Some of those apparitions have become known. Yet, the apparitions seen by those who are Catholic become more public and reach more people all over the world. Catholics, more than people of other religions, recognize me because they are taught to welcome and embrace me.

ANNA: This is a bit confusing to me since when you speak to the Catholic visionaries your messages often contain messages that would only apply to someone following Catholicism. For example, it has been reported that you have said, "Repent, and go to confession." Most religions, on the whole, do not go to a priest to confess their sins. How can that message be for all religions?

MARY: Many things I convey can be confusing when taken literally. Let me explain. The visionaries are following their own belief system, which has already translated many of my words. For instance, when they hear me say "Repent and confess," that has historically meant to "repent and go to confession." This is consistent with their religion. Yet, when I say "Repent and Confess," what I mean, universally, is to be sorry for your transgressions against humanity and God, and ask for forgiveness. If you must go to a church or temple to do so, so be it. If you can learn from your errors and express your sorrow to God directly in prayer, then that is good. Each person must follow the way that is right and perfect for them. It is most important to ask for forgiveness and accept the forgiveness offered, to know that a pardon is given from a good and loving God. Also, along this train of thought, real confession is not only a verbal declaration and admission of a transgression but also a change in the person's behavior and heart. A thief cannot say "I'm sorry for stealing" and then go out and rob someone. I am wandering from the question, but feel this must be said. Do you understand? One will hear my words in a way that is consistent with his or her belief system.

ANNA: Since you "wandered," along these lines, what about penance? The Catholics believe that following confession one must make a penance. Is that true for all people?

MARY: It is true for all people but it isn't necessary to follow one tradition or one religion's way of doing so. The Hindu, Jewish, Muslim, and Buddhist traditions teach that penances must be made to God in order to be forgiven. Penance, in its purest form, is a recognition of the transgression, understanding the reason for the transgression, having an open and contrite heart and a desire to change to be closer to God. The penance practices of various religions differ. The practices of the Hindus, Jews, Muslims, and Buddhists are different from the Catholic tradition but are still good and right. If the practice includes self-introspection and genuine feelings of being sorry, then it is right.

ANNA: How can I be confident of my own filter as I hear you?

MARY: Similar to the messages that I have shared with other people, my words can take on many different meanings depending on the receiver of the message. As long as you are conveying what you are hearing, it is right and good. The people who will be drawn to my words through this book will understand my meaning.

ANNA: You said that you have appeared to people who aren't Catholic or orthodox Christians. How do they know who you are?

MARY: Yes, I have so very many times. They may not see me as Mary, the mother, but they have recognized me as the bearer of Truth. And the Truth is Love and the wisdom of God. You are all connected. God created and belongs to all people. I have appeared as Quan Yin to bring the Truth to all people. My name is not important; it is the message that is.

ANNA: Well, I guess it makes sense that you have to appear in various ways to different people of many different spiritual traditions. Today I met a Catholic man who showed me a photo that he carries with him wherever he goes. The photo contains a superimposed image of you, or at least an image that he recognizes as being you. The image was the traditional depiction that artists have painted through the ages of you; a serene, Caucasian woman with a blue veil. He recognized it as you. He said your image miraculously appeared in the photo. Do you come in that way to people? There have been accounts of people seeing your image on the sides of buildings, in the sky, even in food. Is that a bit overzealous or is there something to it?

MARY: Why would it be overzealous to see me in everything? If an image of me appears in a photo, on a building, or even in a piece of food and gives comfort then I am there. Don't judge my ways. They are as simple and straightforward as I am. I come in many different ways to those who seek me. There is so much judgment in the world. It is time to open up your minds and your hearts. Just admitting "it may be" is a step in the right direction.

ANNA: Does God send you to us or do you come of your own choice?

MARY: It is my purpose to be mother to you all and to help you. God has graced me with this task. I desire to save you all and bring you to inner tranquillity and global peace. I desire to bring Love to all so that you may feel it within yourselves and share it with others. I am a servant of God and delight in spreading his intention and wisdom to the world. I am aligned with God.

ANNA: Why doesn't God just come to us himself?

MARY: God does come to people. Many people hear God and feel the overwhelming presence of love that pervades. Yet, since I was a person and inhabited a body, people are comfortable putting a face to my energy. I have shown myself to people in a way that God has not. No one has seen the face of God. God is a pure vibration that can only be felt. I have been chosen by God to carry his energy and his message in the purest way to all. But I am not the only one. There are many in the heavenly realm that have been coming through to help those on earth. The angels and other spirits are sent to people to help bring about love and peace in the world. I say to all: Listen, feel, and heed my words and the world will be healed! My words are just utterances of the wisdom of God. I come to help teach you so that you can find peace on earth.

ANNA: Do you come to me and others alone?

MARY: I carry the energy of the Creator; his presence is always around me. I also am always surrounded by a host of angels who aid me in helping the world.

ANNA: What do you want to help us do?

MARY: I come to let you know how to find peace and love in the world and to let you know that this must be accomplished. It is the desire of God. I want to help bring forward this love, which will turn the world around and allow peace to flow as it was meant to from the beginning. I come to let people know that they are loved from the highest source and should share this love to find peace.

ANNA: Are you an Ascended Master? (Note to the reader: Ascended Masters are spiritually enlightened beings who, in past incarnations, were just ordinary humans, like most of us. These beings are said to experience a cycle or series of cycles where spiritual transformation takes place and they reach the state of enlightenment.)

MARY: I am an Ascended Master, as are many other souls. I was also chosen by God to bring the Truth forward as the mother. I am the blue vibration of truth. I am the Queen of Angels and heaven. I am here, as the other masters in spirit and the angels, to teach and enlighten my children and lead all to the kingdom. I pray that my messages will be heard and the world find love and peace.

ANNA: Do all people have the ability to attain the spiritual enlightenment of an Ascended Master?

MARY: Of course, all people are equal. This is a long discussion, but I will make it brief. What separates people is their alignment with God and the level of their soul's evolution. As people become more and more spiritual and live the way of Love, they walk into the wisdom of the ages, the wisdom of God and spiritual enlightenment will follow. At the end, the souls of the universe will all be Ascended Masters.

ANNA: Is that what human beings are striving for on a soul level?

MARY: The soul strives to be as perfect as possible to be able to live in unity with God. If the soul can experience and give great love, show compassion, and receive compassion, if it manages to not be fearful of speaking the truth, then the soul will reach the state of purity of an Ascended Master. At that point, the light of Divinity fills the soul and the soul will shine with the love of God.

ANNA: Why are you coming through to us so strongly now?

MARY: The people of the world are ready. Many are seeking the Truth. They no longer want to live in fear. They want to believe and live more closely with God, but are lost. I am here not only to reach out to the believers but to those who are lost or seeking the right path. The world is fragmented and there are many people wandering with nowhere to go. They have been lost in the materialism of the world; greed and lust for tangible objects. Your leaders are lacking the moral integrity to guide their countries to peace and brotherhood among all people. The weapons now are of mass destruction and create fear and unrest. I come to lead people on a path that is free of pain of the world. I come to heal.

Meditation for Chapter One

✦ Gently close your eyes and breathe. Ask the angels to surround you in a brilliant circle of light, love, and protection. Imagine a column of light from heaven moving into the crown of your head, spreading through your body, and anchoring you to the core of the earth. Feel this wonderful light moving through your spinal column up from the tips of your toes. Allow your body to relax as you focus on your breath. Be aware of the rise and fall of your chest as you breathe in all that is good and right in the universe. Be aware that you are filling your lungs with the Divine breath of God. Imagine your breath as a gentle wave moving back and forth and back and forth. Feel your body relax after each exhale as you release stress, negativity, and all else that doesn't serve you. Be conscious of how wonderful this feels. It is truly a gift to permit relaxation and peace into your mind, body, and soul.

✦ Allow the energy of Mary, of her love and peace, to
enter your body with each inhale. Exhale all that
doesn't serve you: all stress, anxiety, anger, animosity,
self-recrimination, and anything else that might get
in the way of connecting to heaven. As you move
into that wonderful place of total relaxation, begin to
feel a sensation of peace moving through your body.
It feels wonderful. Bask in this peace and relax. As
you continue to feel the rise and fall of your chest as
you breathe, imagine there is a silky pale blue light
encircling your body. You feel its gentle vibration as it
swirls around you, alerting and filling your senses. Just
allow yourself to be, as this blue vibration floats around
you. Know that it is good. Let this vibration hug you
gently. Recognize this vibration to be Mother Mary.
Let her warm presence move your focus from your
breath to the soft beating of your heart. Envision your
heart becoming larger in your chest as you let her in.
See the soft blue that is circling around you ease into
your physical body and your heart. Imagine that your
whole being is reaching out to her. As you allow the soft
blue light to fill your heart, recognize that both you and
Mary are blending energetically; you are becoming one
essence. Delight in knowing that you are vibrating with
her energy. As you breathe, begin to feel her more and
more and allow yourself to go deeper. Now imagine a
clear space, free of thought, and allow your breath to
wander in silence (I like to refer to this space as your *soul
space*). Visualize Mary standing in front of you; whatever
image that works best for you is fine. She can continue

to be the pale blue light or a feeling, or perhaps you may want to personify her. Again whatever seems right or feels right.

✦ See her reaching out her hand or see her energy expanding toward you, and hear her saying, "Come follow me on a journey of love." Take her hand, with an open heart. You are now ready to go where she leads. Take a few deep breaths, in through the nose, out through the mouth or nose; whatever feels right. Remain in her presence for a few moments, or as long as you desire.

2

What Is a Soul?

Understanding What We Cannot See

ANNA: Mother, your words are so enlightening. I know that I speak for all when I say thank you for sharing your wisdom with us.

MARY: It is with a heart full of love that I come to raise the vibration of the world and teach all people about love and how to be one with Love.

ANNA: You say that you come to teach us how to be one with Love. Since that is not a physical possibility, how can that happen?

MARY: There are no words that can adequately explain but I will try because you so desire the knowledge. It is difficult because there isn't language to sufficiently convey "emotion" or "feeling." Being one with Love cannot be physical, yet you may feel it in your physical body. Your heart may pick up a beat, you may feel tingling in your abdomen, but Love is a state of being; an emotional state that transcends all that is physical, yet is a part

of the physical world. I know this is confusing . . . The mountains, seas, the sky, and all in the physical realm were created
out of love and show the hand of God in the magnificence of
its beauty. Yet, love has more to do with what the eyes cannot
see . . . For instance, when you witness your child being kind
to another child, you may be affected positively by what you are
seeing. You may describe the feeling as your heart bursting with
love. Yet, this feeling, this love, cannot be held in your hand any
more than you can hold joy in your hand. This love is held in
your very being, as an invisible force that propels you to experience absolute joy. Love is a feeling that holds the highest, most
powerful and purest vibration. So, you may be able to see God
everywhere in creation and know his love by what he made,
but it is the feeling of Love that exceeds the visual. The mountains may be destroyed but the love that it took to create them
remains. Look around you, and feel and know that God and his
love is in everything. Philosophers have been trying to define
love for eons. Love is God. That is what it is. You will know
the energy of the Creator when you open your heart to him and
become aware of him in your life. When you find and recognize
God, the energy of pure Love will unite within you through
your heart and through your soul. This union, or marriage with
Divinity, is the most magnificent act you can ever engage in as
a person, and a feeling that is beyond any emotion that can be
experienced on earth.

ANNA: This is a bit difficult to comprehend since as humans we
are only aware of our physical bodies and what we see and our
mind translates. I will have to think about what you are saying.

MARY: There is a gnostic knowing in your soul that understands
what I am conveying. Rest in my words and let your soul bring
you the wisdom that you seek. It will be done if you so desire.

ANNA: We were created in the image of God. You say God is the embodiment of love, that God is Love. But we are made of flesh and bone. How can we connect with God through our souls? And what is a soul?

MARY: When used to better yourself and the world, the mind is so wonderful! I am pleased by your questions. Imagine that people are souls, the energy of God, covered with flesh. Your bodies are intricate machines that defy science over and over. Only the greatest intelligence could have created humans and all creatures. God is that being of the highest intelligence. Your body should be taken care of, as it is a gift that allows the soul to achieve union with the perfect love. The soul holds the energy and vibration of God and can recognize it within itself and within the total embodiment of the energy in God. The soul is that which yearns for God because it knows God. The yearning can be so great that people have a conscious recognition of it at times. The human soul is the part of you that is not physical, yet it represents the majority of who you are. You are all so much more than what you see and feel! Again, this is difficult to understand, I know. The soul is all, yet it is separate. It is the vibration and energy of the person. It is the part of every human being that lasts eternally after the body experiences death.

ANNA: I guess, there is proof in the Bible that people have souls. In Genesis 35:18 there is a description of the death of Rachel, Jacob's wife, saying she named her son "as her soul was departing."

MARY: The soul is all that exists after death and carries the "self" of the person who is accountable for its actions during its life on earth.

ANNA: So people aren't really human? We are souls with a covering. Interesting . . .

MARY: I am human no more. Someday, you will no longer be human. The soul will always exist. It chooses the body to incarnate into so that it can learn its lessons. It chooses its genetics and family in order to do so. The soul influences the mind as each part of the human machine is integrated with the soul. It also influences free will. It is not separate but part of all that is human. Life can be an extraordinary experience and should be relished and enjoyed as God wants it to be. God desires you all to be living in abundance. Once the soul passes from the body and the soul goes through its life review, there is peace. The emotions of hate and fear don't exist. Once in the Divine realm there is no need for supremacy and the things of the world; there is no battle with the body and the human condition. The soul is content to be in a place of pure love. Each soul has a personality and is unique, yet they exist without the need to dominate. All praise and glory goes to God; not to each other. But one must complete their soul mission before any of this can be accomplished.

ANNA: People have said that they feel their souls leaving them as they sleep. Is this true? Can our souls just take off and leave the sleeping body and "astral travel"? There is a saint I admire whose name is Padre Pio. There are accounts of him being in more than one place at one time although he was lying in his bed in Italy. There are thousands of letters from people saying that they saw him and he allowed God's healing to flow from his hands to them and they were healed. And so, he could be sound asleep in Italy while people in Texas, England, and other places in the world were seeing him and being healed by him. Is it true that his soul left his body and traveled spiritually to complete his mission to heal people?

MARY: Padre Pio was a special human being. He understood with infinite wisdom the workings of the soul. He was of a pure heart, and devoted to God and his own mission of bringing the love of God to the world through miraculous healing. God worked through his soul as Pio traveled the world to heal those in need.

ANNA: This is so fascinating to me. Maybe that is why so many people wake up tired in the morning . . . maybe their souls are working hard and it is exhausting for them!

MARY: It may be . . . the soul affects the body and the body the soul. Remember the body is the glove covering the soul. If the glove has a tear the soul is affected, if the soul is not at ease, the glove is manipulated and may not be comfortable. And so it goes . . .

ANNA: Do our souls retain our personalities even after death and through lifetimes?

MARY: Yes, people do retain their personalities. It is a big part of who they are. Many personalities may be similar but your personality is unique unto you. Upon reaching the realm, the energy of the person loses the anger, the hate, and the animosity, among other negative feelings, and displays joy and love. The soul is able to be filled with the positive aspects of their personality and it continues. Someone who was funny in life carries their sense of humor to the other side. Someone who was carefree is still carefree. And when they come through to visit their loved ones on earth their personalities are recognizable.

ANNA: So that is the reason why when I feel those on the other side, I sometimes feel their personalities as they reveal them to me. Many times they also tell me what they believe in and what they like and don't like.

MARY: Yes and so when you pass on the information, it is a validation.

ANNA: How can we know our soul's mission?

MARY: Ask and you will receive the knowledge. Each one of you is uniquely gifted. Recognize your gifts; there is a reason that you are gifted in the way that you are. Within your gifts, recognize your passion and what you so enjoy doing. Through these you will find your mission and your purpose. I say to you, don't deny your gifts or your passions. They were bestowed upon you as blessings. No blessing is better or worse than any other. And, collectively, all people were born to heal themselves and each other. You are all healers.

ANNA: So, if I understand correctly, no matter what our gifts are, they weren't randomly given to us. They are a part of how we are to complete our soul mission? So, for example, if someone's gift is excelling at baseball and is doing so professionally, that is part of his soul mission. Interesting . . . On another note, what is the difference between the mind and the soul?

MARY: Your soul never truly leaves you; it is always connected to your being. Yet, the soul doesn't sleep or rest. And so, when you sleep your soul may go to a different dimension to teach, heal, or learn. By doing so, it can better help you as a person following your path. Sometimes people will dream about these travels of their souls.

ANNA: You talk about the soul going off to teach, learn, or heal. I have read that astral projection and out-of-body experiences are part of many of the mystical traditions and underlie most of the major religions. The ancient Egyptians believed that the "Ka" or soul can leave the body and travel at will. It is all so fascinating that people have believed this to be true for many centuries but now we seem to just be learning about it.

MARY: And so is the way of the world. As people become more and more intelligent there is a need to prove scientifically all that occurs. Many things cannot be proven so easily. Someday it may all be proven by science, but not yet.

ANNA: Are the mind and the soul different?

MARY: The mind and soul are similar, yet so different. The soul is the spiritual nature of humankind but it has the ability to have thoughts; it can act and feel. The mind is the place where people think, reason, and retain knowledge. The soul is the essence of each person and contains the vibration and essence of God while the mind is in charge of a person's consciousness and thoughts. They work with each other.

ANNA: I guess the real question is "where does the mind exist?" We know where the brain is, but is that really the mind? And are the mind and soul both a part of one another?

MARY: The mind and the brain work together but are two separate entities. The brain is physical and part of the body, whereas the mind is an extension of the soul. Within the mind are all our memories, our morals, conscious and nonconscious thoughts, feelings of love, anger, joy, disenchantment. The brain, when healthy, allows an individual to go into the mind and make sense of the world. When something is amiss with the brain, it affects the ability to access things in the mind to bring them into consciousness. The mind exists outside of the brain but works with it. The soul is the place where intuition and gnostic wisdom reside.

ANNA: This reminds me of what René Descartes argues in his theory of dualism. He maintained that there is a two-way interaction between the mind and brain.

MARY: Yes, philosophers have sought for centuries to explain this and many have been correct. Descartes was right in his assertions.

ANNA: You mention gnostic knowledge; what is that?

MARY: Gnostic knowledge is the spiritual wisdom that resides on a conscious level, yet comes from the soul. So this wisdom is held by the soul and shared with the mind. The brain, through its intricate functioning, allows this knowledge to be processed and, thus, known to the person.

ANNA: So we are born with an "all knowing." If this is true, why do we turn away from it?

MARY: This brings us to free will.

ANNA: Are you saying that the mind, the soul, and the brain work together but are separate?

MARY: Yes, the body, both the physical and nonphysical; the etheric and subtle bodies as well as the organs are all part of God's creation. God masterfully allowed the human form to be completely and mechanically perfect in its ability to be in both the natural and supernatural/spiritual realms. You are all magnificent and can live by combining all these aspects of your being! Take care of your physical body and worship it as it serves your soul. Exercise your soul through prayer and meditation. By doing so, you will find a sense of satisfaction and reverence to the Creator.

ANNA: So I guess we all have the ability to be clairvoyant and intuitive?

MARY: Of course you all do! This is part of every human being. Some souls are more spiritually evolved and more trusting of God, and able to allow the intuition or wisdom to emerge. It is fear that blocks intuition. Recognize that you were created by Love, not fear. All that you possess physically and on a soul level should be honored and used for the highest good of God, yourself, and others.

ANNA: Very cool . . . Can the soul be good or evil?

MARY: By its very nature, simply because the soul returns to the earth to fix the issues of its past lives or to help others, it can only be good. If the mind ignores the influences of the soul and the essence of Divinity, actions may follow that may not be good and right.

ANNA: Does the soul have a gender?

MARY: The soul has no gender. It will occupy a body which has a gender, but the soul is a vibration like that of God. The soul may reincarnate as male or female over the course of lifetimes.

ANNA: Spirits generally show themselves to me as male or female, when they come through. Why is that?

MARY: That is for your sake and the purpose of communicating to those who are living. How else would there be validation? How else could you describe them? You can describe in concrete terms what you can see.

ANNA: This conversation is fascinating. A wonderful thought; it is all so heady. Do you think that people may be able to embrace these concepts and perhaps accept that we are really souls?

MARY: Yes, the soul of each person wants to be known. It is not of utmost importance to understand the differences between the soul, mind, and brain. It is more important to just realize that all are soul beings, not just human beings. Because the soul is not physical or visible it is difficult for some people to understand its nature. Yet, there are people who can see the soul in colors surrounding people or feel its density. There has been more and more talk of this ability to see the soul aura over the last fifty years. The world is ready to accept this. It is time. It is important to know above all else said that you are all souls who share a vibration with God and that vibration is Love. Simple, but it is Truth.

ANNA: Do you think people are just so wrapped up with "being human" and living life that they just don't care about their souls?

MARY: Yes, this is sad but true. Heed my words my children, love and honor your soul for it is the essence of who you are! It is your connection to the Almighty and the one true Love. It will lead you to all that is good. It carries the energy and vibration of God within you all.

ANNA: This is so fascinating. I'd like to return to who we are as people. What is the correct way of defining ourselves? If we are just flesh and bone covering the essence of who we really are, should we say we are souls?

MARY: Oh, my daughter, why the need to define? You are all these things! If someone hits you, you will experience physical pain; if someone mocks you, you will experience emotional pain; if you go against your spiritual nature and God, your soul will weep and try to bring you back to God.

ANNA: Let's talk about mental illness and physical handicaps. How are we to understand and cope with it?

MARY: Good question. Prior to the soul reincarnating, it is fully aware of the challenges it must endure to learn lessons not acquired in prior lifetimes. And so, the soul accepts new handicaps to learn from them and to teach those around it. It may be painful on a human level; but it is accepted on a soul level. By doing so, by living through the handicap, not only can the soul evolve but it can also allow other souls to evolve. All humans are handicapped in some capacity.

ANNA: How can other souls learn and evolve through someone else's handicap?

MARY: The souls in heaven communicate with each other and make "pacts" with each other regarding what they need to learn when they return to earth. So, a group of souls may decide the best way for them to learn from each other. Someone who is handicapped teaches those around him compassion, patience, servitude, and understanding.

ANNA: But what about those who are severely mentally ill, or abusive emotionally or physically to other people? I'm thinking of schizophrenia or psychosis.

MARY: Sometimes the lesson for those around such an individual is to have compassion; to recognize the human imperfection and love the person anyway. This is very difficult. But know that the mental illness is not related to evil, or taking on the burden of the wrongdoings of humankind. In addition to teaching other souls, the reason for mental illness and other handicaps is often related to bringing into balance or "fixing" the wrongs in a past life or learning what was not learned in other lifetimes of the person or persons around the ill person.

ANNA: Is the soul trying to correct itself?

MARY: Yes, it is. For instance, it may be that in a previous life a person was cruel to those that were handicapped. Perhaps they come back as the one who is handicapped to understand their own lack of compassion and wrongdoings. Also, the family around that handicapped or mentally ill person is also "fixing" their wrongdoings from a past life by caring for this person who is handicapped. These are all lessons. Sometimes there isn't true clarity until life is over and in the place of all knowing with God.

ANNA: Before, you mentioned that the heart and soul work together. When you speak of the heart, is that the same as the soul?

MARY: The heart, in symbolic terms, is the center of love. In the physical body, it is also the organ that is affected most by an abundance or lack of love. It is the energy center of love. The human body is intricate and each organ in the body has many different purposes. It is also the place that is most associated with the soul. Yet, the soul doesn't reside in the heart, nor the heart in the soul. Just like the brain, they are separate yet a part of each other. The soul encompasses your whole being; what is both in your body and in your energy field.

ANNA: What do you mean that the soul is in our energy fields?

MARY: Your energy field is simply your vibration. The soul vibrates and so it is a part of your energy field. Your energy field is a part of your makeup. I am repeating, I know, but this is a difficult concept for people. Feel my words, absorb them and you will understand.

ANNA: This is difficult to understand. I'm not sure I understand what you are saying! But I need to know more . . . Does the soul come through, knowing how its life will turn out?

MARY: No, the soul learns and lives on earth through the actions and reactions of its human form. There is no fate; only journeys. It is all unwritten. Yet, the soul comes through knowing what it must learn and influences the mind (again which is part of it) to choose one path or another. It acts as a compass of sorts for the mind.

ANNA: So when we die, does the soul carry on? And what of the body?

MARY: The body once dead is nothing. The body decomposes and is turned to dust. It goes back to a form of nothingness. It disintegrates and goes back to the earth. People build mausoleums to give respect to the dead person's physical body, yet the body is insignificant. It is the soul that goes on.

ANNA: What if the soul does not fulfill its mission?

MARY: The soul is given the option to come back to the earth and try to learn again. In the course of our spiritual evolution people acquire the ability of reaching spiritual bliss. Every one of us is at a different stage of spiritual evolution and the experience of bliss is related to where the person is in their spiritual evolution.

ANNA: What is spiritual bliss?

MARY: When the soul feels total joy and happiness, and is free from the constraints of the body and its pain.

ANNA: What is spiritual evolution?

MARY: That is a complex question. The purpose of the soul's returning to earth over many ages is to learn to be more like God and be in perfect union with God. It is the balance in the soul of knowledge, wisdom, compassion, love for God, faith in God, awareness of God, and rejection of all that is not of God. In the beginning of the evolution of the soul, the soul is ignorant concerning its nature and perceives only through the five senses. As the soul evolves through lifetimes, there is an awakening to more of the esoteric nature and a consciousness of this process. The soul continues until it reaches bliss.

ANNA: Does the soul have any memory of past lives? Why don't humans remember?

MARY: Yes, the soul remembers all. It is difficult for the soul to come back to life on earth after being in the Divine realm. Yet, the soul innately loves God and chooses to learn what it didn't learn in past lives. It also strives to reach a deeper connection with God that can only be achieved by reliving on earth.

ANNA: Do all souls reincarnate?

MARY: Jesus did not reincarnate, as he lived and died in perfection. I didn't reincarnate because I could better serve by helping people from my place in the heavenly realm. Yet, all other souls reincarnate.

ANNA: Can you tell me more about reincarnation?

MARY: Every time the soul reenters this world there is a Divine purpose. Those that follow Kabbalah call this "gilgul haneshamot," or the cycling of the soul. The Hindus explain that reincarnation is the natural way the soul evolves from immaturity to spiritual illumination, and that the soul is immortal but inhabits one body after another on the earth during its evolutionary journey. Again, it is to learn what it didn't learn in past incarnations. Its purpose is to reach a state of purity to share in the perfect love that is God.

ANNA: But why can't the soul just learn its lessons while being in the Divine realm?

MARY: The Divine realm is beyond anything experienced on earth because all exist in a state of pure unconditional love and peace, which makes it perfect. God fills his realm with his energy which is unmarred and flawless. There is no wrong, only right. The soul needs to return to an imperfect place, a place filled with good and bad, right and wrong, to "fix" the mistakes and the transgressions made in previous lives. The soul is given another chance to redeem itself. For the most part, the soul may have the same challenges to which it succumbed in its previous life and is given a chance to overcome them.

There are some souls who do not return for their own growth or perfection but rather to benefit others. This can be to help out an individual or a large number of people. This is usually an evolved soul who does so. It is with great compassion and love that this is done.

ANNA: Mother, if we are here to learn lessons and to correct past mistakes, it would make sense if we could remember our past lives and fix it all this time around. But most people do not remember their past lives. It seems like an agreement of sorts . . . So have we agreed to forget our past lives and why?

MARY: My daughter, you are seeking the logic as a human being, but it is beyond that, it is so much more. Not remembering past lives frees people to make different choices. They may enter new relationships and choose different directions in life to expand and evolve as a soul instead of living in a way that they recognize and is comfortable. Do you understand?

ANNA: I think so . . . so if someone harmed me in a past life, I might not be able to let it go in my current life and maybe even try to get even?

MARY: That is right. Also, God desires that your lessons are truly learned. So if you forget your past life you are free to learn your lessons without any knowledge of what you did in a previous life.

ANNA: So, if I was a horrible ruler in a past life who controlled people with fear I may need to come back to learn not to be mean, controlling, and authoritarian in dealing with people.

MARY: Yes, and by not remembering past lives, the present life is much easier. Too much information from the past lives would complicate your current life. You would be meeting people who you have known in other lifetimes whose relationship with you is different in the present lifetime. It would compromise your soul pact to help each other learn and evolve in different situations assuming different relationship roles. This would be so confusing! Your mother from a past life may now be your daughter. You may psychologically reverse roles if you recognized her as your mother from another life. It would be so complex.

ANNA: I think I get it now. Mother, you previously spoke of perfection. What do you mean by perfection?

MARY: The soul seeks perfect love for God. This involves loving yourself and others without judgment and without boundaries. It also means honoring God above all things. It is not a physical perfect, it is a perfect that is beyond that. It is all about joining in absolute love and vibration with God. It is difficult to reach this state outside the realm of heaven, but it can be done. When your love for God motivates you to live your life focusing on what he wants for you and the world, when you put love and compassion for all people including yourself first and foremost because you recognize his energy in all people, your love will reach the highest vibration and perfectly mingle with his love. That is what reaching this perfect state that the soul longs for really is. You cannot love anyone but God in this way. This state which creates perfect love supersedes all other love known to humankind. Only God who is consistent in being the "I Am" can accept and give back this love. His love is always perfect.

ANNA: You used the term the "I Am" in referring to God. Can you tell me what it means?

MARY: I am so pleased to share this with you. You will see the beauty and magnificence of "I Am." As written in the Old Testament, Moses said to God, "Suppose I go to the Israelites and say to them, 'The God of your fathers has sent me to you,' and they ask me, 'What is his name?' Then what shall I tell them?"

God said to Moses, "I AM WHO I AM. This is what you are to say to the Israelites: 'I AM has sent me to you.'" What God is conveying is his absolute reality beyond all others. His name is insignificant, he just is. There is no beginning of his energy and no end. He simply is the power that is. Also, since God is not determined by a force outside of himself, implicit in the "I Am" is his consistent nature. He doesn't change. He doesn't qualify the "I Am"; it just is. So when Moses goes back to his people to speak of this power that came to him, he doesn't need to qualify it either. Because there are no qualifiers, the "I Am" never changes. For instance, you may say "I am hungry." But after you take your meal, that sentence is not valid anymore for then you can say "I am not hungry." Also, "I Am" signifies his great power. "I Am" therefore I am an energy that never grows weary, is never less than what "I Am." Also, when God says *I AM THAT I AM*, he removes our objectivity. No one needs to have a different view of God. He can be no different than what he is. He doesn't change to fit people; he is the same energy to all. Because he is the "I Am," he does not conform to us; rather we must accept his energy as perfect and right just the way it is.

ANNA: Wow, that's amazing that two simple words mean so much! What about soul mates. Do they really exist?

MARY: Souls reincarnate in clusters or soul groups to support each other and teach each other. On a physical level there may even be a subtle recognition of knowing someone although on a physical level this can be a first meeting. Sometimes, two souls are reincarnated that have reincarnated over the ages many times and are energetically joined together. That would be a soul mate. Yet, it isn't necessarily a romantic relationship or energy. It is simply a support of one another. And, souls may have more than one soul mate.

ANNA: You mentioned that we make pacts with other souls. Do we come back again and again with the same souls and soul groups?

MARY: Yes, over eons you will reincarnate again and again with the same souls. There is understanding in such a group of souls. You will play different roles in the group. Over time you may be the mother, father, son, or friend to another soul.

ANNA: This is so amazing! So how can people be in touch with their souls?

MARY: People must pray and meditate. Ask that God allow for the messages of the soul to come through. People may also ask their soul to show them their path and the right acts to engage in for their journey in life.

ANNA: Will you teach us how to pray?

MARY: It's my heart's desire.

Meditation for Chapter Two

✦ Gently close your eyes and breathe. Ask the angels to surround you in a brilliant circle of light, love, and protection. Imagine a column of light from heaven moving into the crown of your head, spreading through your body, and anchoring you to the core of the earth. Feel this wonderful light moving through your spinal column up from the tips of your toes. Allow your body to relax as you focus on your breath. Be aware of the rise and fall of your chest as you breathe in all that is good and right in the universe. Be aware that you are filling your lungs with the Divine breath of God. Imagine your breath as a gentle wave moving back and forth and back and forth. Feel your body relax after each exhale as you release stress, negativity, and all else that doesn't serve you. Be conscious of how wonderful this feels. It is truly a gift to permit relaxation and peace into your mind, body, and soul.

+ Allow the energy of Mary, of her love and peace, to enter your body with each inhale. Exhale all stress, anxiety, anger, animosity, self-recrimination, and anything else that might get in the way of connecting to heaven. As you move into that wonderful place of total relaxation, begin to feel a sensation of peace moving through your body. It feels wonderful. Bask in this relaxation and peace. As you continue to feel the rise and fall of your chest as you breathe, imagine there is a silky, pale blue light encircling your body. You feel its gentle vibration as it swirls around you, alerting and filling your senses. Just allow yourself to be. Know that it is good. Let this vibration hug you gently. Recognize this vibration to be Mother Mary. Let her warm presence move your focus from your breath to the soft beating of your heart.

+ Envision your heart becoming larger in your chest as you let her in. See the soft blue that is circling around you ease into your physical body and your heart. Imagine that your whole being is reaching out to her, to be a part of her. As you allow the soft blue light to fill your heart, recognize that both you and Mary are blending energetically; you are becoming one essence. Delight in knowing that you are vibrating with her energy. As you breathe, begin to feel her more and more and allow yourself to go deeper. Now imagine a clear space, free of thought, and allow your breath to wander in silence. Visualize Mary standing in front of you; whatever image that works best for you is fine. She can continue to be the pale blue light or a feeling, or perhaps you may want to personify her. Again, whatever seems right or feels right. See her reaching out her hand or see her energy expanding toward you.

+ She shows you a reflection of your soul in the mirror. Hear Mary say, "This is the real you, the one that was made in the image of God." You may see your soul in whatever way it wishes to appear to you; sometimes people see a beautiful light, others report seeing a simple version of their physical self. Know that there is no right reflection. As you stand in front of this mirror, you may want to ask questions of your soul. You may want to ask your soul for guidance, for healing, or to present itself to you more clearly in your daily life. Notice any feelings, either physical or emotional, taking place in your body. Sit with your soul for however long you desire and know that God is protecting you and allowing wisdom to be brought to you.

3

Pray with Me

What Is Prayer?
What Is the Right Way to Pray?

ANNA: Mother, why is it your desire that we pray?

MARY: It is a direct way of communicating with God. God adores it when his children come to him. When you pray, you are consciously including God in your life. God is full of joy when you invite him in!

ANNA: If God knows all, why does he need to hear what we say?

MARY: Why does your husband have to tell you that he loves you? Don't you know already? It isn't a matter of what you are praying for, but rather the act of coming before the greatest power and connecting to his healing energy or simply thanking him for the abundance in your life. By doing so your faith increases, and your desire to be with God grows. This is also a surrender of control as you place your wants and needs in God's hands. For example, if your husband tells you he loves you but his actions speak differently, you know your relationship is lacking. The same is true when you pray. Prayer must coincide with the way in which you live. In that way, your daily life becomes a living prayer as well.

ANNA: But how can my life become a living prayer?

MARY: You must walk with God, not just talk to him. You must recognize him in all that you do and all that you feel and see. Your actions must be consistent with the love he sends to you. It is not just in receiving the miracles through prayer, but being a conduit of God's love toward yourself and others. Don't be like those who pretend to pray on bended knee, saying words of adoration to God but treating others in horrible ways.

ANNA: I understand . . . we must be godlike and not just "talk the talk," but "walk the walk!" You mention surrendering. Does that mean that once a prayer is said, and if there is surrendering, we can just leave it all in God's hands and do nothing?

MARY: Surrendering does not mean relinquishing responsibility. When you surrender, you may give up some control. God will partner with you to allow your prayers to be answered. He will direct you. You are strong and intelligent and must use these attributes as God leads you. You will know. Humans are intuitive people who can feel and discern. Don't ignore this "knowing." Coupled with the power of God, you will find the answers. God will bring people and situations to you so that your prayers can be realized. In prayer, you awaken a piece of your being to be able to travel with God and find the answers you so desire.

ANNA: How should the world pray?

MARY: Each person would do well to seek this answer in his or her heart. The best prayer is one that combines the entire heart, soul, mind, and being. This will allow for the surrender of will to God. In doing so, the vibration of the one who is praying is raised to the level of the Divine vibration. In prayer you must give by emptying yourself to the Lord. As I am a vessel for Divinity, so are all people. Pray by believing in what you pray for. With faith it will be received. Even if you stop momentarily during the day to say a simple word to God, it is a prayer; a recognition on your part that you live in union with God. Be in union with God and with me as you go about your day and your life. Again, always pray in pure faith believing that your prayers will be answered. Always pray in gratitude. Begin each prayer with "Thank you, God . . ." for God is magnificent and desires your acknowledgment that all good comes from him.

ANNA: You say that the "best prayer is one that combines the entire heart, soul, mind, and being." I think I do that, but how can I be sure? How can I truly know?

MARY: I know this can be difficult to understand. The human race is complex by God's design. You are all made of an intellect, a soul, a heart, and a being. Your being is your body and your essence or soul. In praying with all of these parts, you use words to speak with God and express your worship, gratitude, and desires; open up your soul to speak silent words to God; allow your heart to unlock and receive. Also allow your heart to give love to God, which invigorates your senses and your body and essence. This will help you feel connected to the energy of God. In prayer your vibration raises to the highest level and you are in the presence of the Almighty sharing one energy as all of these aspects of your person work in congruence. How wonderful! If all people could understand this, the world would be constantly praying! The mind has the ability to connect to the soul through prayer and allow the soul to sing praises to the Lord! This is a state of grace. Yet, don't be dissuaded to pray if it takes time to get to this state: Patience, intent, love, and sincerity will bring you there. Never give up. All people can reach this place of sanctuary with the Lord. When you pray, leave the conscious world behind and be present with God. Try not to think but feel. Empty your-self as you open your heart and soul to God. Intend it to be so, and it will. As you begin to pray, you may feel anxiety being released from your body and a feeling of peace overcome you. That feeling occurs as you surrender and give yourself to God. God, in return, will fill you with a feeling of pure peace. That is what praying with your whole being feels like. Also, the inten-tion of doing so is right and good with God and he will lead you to opening yourself to prayer with every piece of who you are. It is how I prayed and how I pray now. I am a being that carries the light of the Divine within. I was that being while I was living and am now. I surrendered completely to that Power. I prayed in faith. All humans have that same ability.

ANNA: How does one pray in faith? I thought prayer increases our faith not the other way around.

MARY: It is both, my dear. By believing that you are worthy to communicate with God and that your prayers are heard and will be answered is an act of faith. This will, by its very nature, increase your faith in God as the omnipresent power that answers prayers. Don't begin praying by pleading and begging to God, but rather by thanking God that your prayers will be realized. An act of faith comes from claiming the answers to your prayers without the validation of seeing them realized. You must know that God loves you and wants you to live in joy and abundance of spirit. God does not want to punish you or make you beg at his feet. God is loving and good, and as his creation, as a part of his energy, you are worthy to have your prayers answered. Prayers are like flower buds in the beginning of spring, reaching up to heaven, allowing the light to bring forth growth. Of course, prayers must be for the good of yourself and all the world. Prayers cannot be to hurt or hinder another person or creature. Prayers must come from the heart and soul, not the ego. Here is a suggestion on how you may pray: *Thank you, God, for all blessings that I have seen and those yet to be seen. In faith, I welcome all blessings that are for my highest good and the highest good of my family, friends, and the entire world. With great love for you, my Lord, thank you for the joy and happiness that I have experienced as well as the joy and happiness that is to come. Thank you for helping me to grow and learn from my pain. I open my heart to receive all that you are sending to me, my family, and friends.* This is a simple prayer that speaks from the heart of gratitude and love. Most people complicate prayer; try to keep it simple. Pray from your heart. And when you have no words, give all that is in your heart up to God by saying *My Lord, you know what is in my heart. I lift it up to you as I don't have the words to communicate all that I wish to give to you in prayer.* Sit silently after praying and allow God to come through to you in whatever way seems perfect. You may feel a calmness overtake you or a feeling of undeniable love. You may even hear words that provide answers. I desire you all to open your hearts and feel the energy and love of God as he moves through you.

ANNA: Although the prayer you just gave me is not a specific prayer, I understand that we may claim answers to specific issues in prayer. For example, thank you for the gift of my daughter finding a partner who will love and honor her. Am I correct in believing that this prayer could occur before the partner has materialized in the present moment?

MARY: Yes, that is a prayer of faith. You do not actually see the manifestation and realization of the answer as you are praying, yet you believe in the power of God so much that you will claim the answer in advance.

ANNA: What is the difference between a prayer and an intention?

MARY: Words! Words can be confusing. As to prayer and intention, all depends on how you are using them. When prayer and intention are used together you combine your energy with that of God and recognize that it is only by cocreating with God that your prayers become reality. I know that can be confusing so let me explain: An intention includes your ego and manifesting your desires. Yet, it doesn't happen without the power of the Divine. When prayer and intentions are combined, you end up partnering with God. You claim the intention in prayer as answered, and you give up the ego control and move into the energy of God and let God create along with you. As you manifest your intentions with prayer, you are acting in faith. By doing so, you combine the highest vibration of your own and cocreate with God. You are creations of God; you are an extension of his love, and all are worthy.

ANNA: So many people pray to you and others in heaven. Is that right? Should people pray to you as well as to God?

MARY: No, ask me and I will pray with you. I am not the One who answers prayers, I am the intermediary who makes your prayers stronger on their way to the Creator. I can help open your eyes to the miracles around you if you ask, but I cannot design the miracles. I am the handmaiden of the Lord but I am not the Lord. It's the same when you pray with the saints, prophets, angels, or other beings in your religion. They will pray with you.

ANNA: You say that if we believe in faith it will be received, yet people pray all the time and feel their prayers are not answered. How can that be if these prayers were said in faith?

MARY: Oh, my daughter, this is so difficult for people. It breaks my heart to see the pain and the anger at God when prayers are not answered exactly as people want them to be answered. People should never stop praying, but understand that many times what they desire in prayer may not be for their highest good or for the best of the person whom they are praying for. Your prayers are answered by bringing attention to a situation and allowing God to do what is best. God is all knowing and a loving God. I understand the pain that follows an unanswered prayer. I prayed for my son's life to be spared and yet his life ended in a horrible way. I felt helpless and suffered deeply. But, I came to believe that this was not only for Jesus's highest good, but the highest good of the world. This comprehension was a salve on my wounded heart. For the rest of my days and now into eternity, I still pray and know that prayers can be answered.

ANNA: I can't imagine your pain. Were you angry at God? How long after Jesus's death did it take for you to make peace with God?

MARY: I was always at peace with God. Yet, I endured great emotional pain during my son's last days and during his persecution. I witnessed the purity of his love as he spread it to all people even as he was rejected. As a mother and a person who loved him and his message, the way people treated him caused me great pain. I didn't understand fully the true reason for the circumstances of my son's suffering for it wasn't revealed to me until later. Yet, my faith in God never wavered. I was angry at those who tortured him and tormented him. I was angry and frustrated that people could not understand that Jesus came to show them how to save themselves. Instead they killed the one who lived for them. People say that Jesus died for the sins of mankind. That is not totally true. He lived for the sins of mankind; to help teach people how to live and not to sin and transgress against God; and yet they couldn't hear his message. They couldn't see that he only wanted to love them and bring them the peace they were looking for. God did not destroy my son's flesh; men did. As his mother, the one who brought him into the world and loved him as only a mother could, the pain my son endured tore at me and left a piece of me frayed. I grieved for Jesus and longed for him the rest of my days on earth. I went on and lived my life, giving and receiving, smiling and crying, but never forgetting the pain. The pain was housed in my heart, but my life went on. I recognized that life is a gift and must be lived. I lived for my son and my other children and helped spread Jesus's message. At my death, God granted me the release of my feelings of anger and forgiveness. I so loved my son, grieved and missed him. Yet, I recognized within days of his passing that his words and the goodness he spoke of would change my people and the entire world if they would only listen. And so it was and so it is.

ANNA: What role does fate play in unanswered prayers? For example, if I pray that a loved one is healed from sickness yet my prayers go unheeded, does this mean it was fated to be as such?

MARY: My dear one, this is a complicated question. The answer involves faith and releasing control to God. If you pray for healing but it is not in the individual's best interest, the prayer will be answered based on that person's needs. But let me be clear: this isn't fate since fate speaks to predestination. You each have free will, and can change your life as you make decisions. I understand that you are praying, or so you believe, for your loved one's highest good, yet you must have faith that God knows what is best. Pray by surrendering yourself and your loved ones to the will of God. Pray for their highest good. It is an act of pure faith since you are giving control to God and stepping out. All prayers are answered, but not always in the way that you see fit. Have faith and know that your prayers are being heard.

ANNA: This type of praying can be very challenging.

MARY: Yes, it is very difficult to give up control to God. I know this well. I had to give up control to the will of God for my son. Yet, God had a plan that was far above my understanding. You must know that as well.

ANNA: I think many people want to make sure that God answers their prayers in a way that fits what they see as best. They may be frightened of what the answer might be.

MARY: My dear, this fear of God pains me. This fear comes from a belief that God may hurt in some way; it speaks of a lack of love. God is love and all that comes from God represents love. There is no reason to fear. People may not like the answer to the prayer or may not understand the answer at first. Yet, people must trust in God.

ANNA: I have read that fear is the opposite of love. Is that true?

MARY: Yes, the world must know that fear is the opposite of love. In fear there is no love or faith. There is uneasiness and the need to protect oneself. In fear there is a holding back of your energy from mingling with that of God. It separates and leaves one feeling alone and unloved. In love, there is faith and surrender. In love there is comfort. In love there is God. God is love. Fear and love are opposing forces. Do you understand?

ANNA: Yes, I understand but am confused about the use of the word *fear* in the holy texts. In the Bible it speaks of "fearing God." If fear is the opposite of Love, why would God want us to fear him?

MARY: The Bible was written by men and translated from one language to the next. Men understood power and ruled with fear. Generations have ruled with fear. It made sense then, and to some now that if God is a power, then he must be feared for he can destroy you all. These ideas make me so sad for the world. God does not desire to be feared but to be loved and respected. God does not seek to condemn and punish but to love. Love God with all your being; honor him and praise him but don't fear. Fear will push you from a relationship with God. God wants to embrace you all.

ANNA: So if God is love, where does fear come from?

MARY: Fear comes from a place that has the ability to pull you away from God. What pulls you from God is not of the light. I say to you, my children, do not allow fear to move you from love and prayer. Pray with all your heart and know that your God is an energy of perfect love and loves you unconditionally. Your prayers are heard and answered in pure love.

ANNA: Can you elaborate on that place where fear resides?

MARY: Fear resides in each one of you and is manipulated by a lack of control. This lack of control manifests in negative energy that tears you away from God. Fear, anger, depression, anxiety, and inner turmoil grow out of this.

ANNA: Okay. So with that in mind, I am curious about the power of prayer. Does it really have power?

MARY: My daughter, as one connects to the Lord, prayer becomes all powerful. Prayer is not just an uttering of the mind, but when the heart and soul are involved there can be no stronger force on earth. And, when people pray together, the mountains ring with their words and energy and the angels sing along with them. Prayer can be accomplished by all. God is overjoyed when people pray and come to him. He is the Father, the Creator, and wants to come into each person's life. When people pray there is an acknowledgment of the Father-child relationship. Yet, even a solitary prayer holds a tremendous amount of power. It is the sword that protects and cuts through all the problems and evil in the world.

ANNA: Many say prayer is stronger in groups. Is that true?

MARY: Praying in a group is a different experience. When people come together to pray in unison it is like music to heaven. As they pray they are uniting with each other, and each person adds to the strength of the prayer. Yet, praying alone and emptying your heart also has its merits and strength. Your prayers in solitude are special; by doing so you begin to recognize that your soul can rise up to speak. Both ways are honored and heard by God. When you pray alone ask me, the angels, the mystics, prophets, and saints to pray with you. Your prayers will gather the strength and power of heaven as they are brought to the feet of God.

ANNA: I have heard about studies suggesting that when people pray for an ill person there are more occurrences of healing than in instances for when no one is praying. Is this true?

MARY: This *is* true, my dear one.

ANNA: Does this mean that if we truly, collectively pray for world peace, it really could be possible?

MARY: Yes, yes, yes! I have come and will continue to come to people to tell them to pray for peace, and yes, the world can be saved. But, the prayers must be followed with action: compassion and love for all people must be demonstrated. More people need to pray for peace and become more loving toward each other. I am the Queen of Peace for all people. I don't speak of peace for only a select few but for the world. Continue to pray for peace and to act in a way that promotes unity and love and the world will be healed. Start out by praying for peace in your family, community, country, and then the world. See visions of the world at peace. Pray for peace of heart, mind, and spirit, and that healing will spread from person to person. Pray for a change that will end fighting and terrorism and suffering. The battle for peace will be won but all must pray and live according to the laws of Love.

ANNA: What are the laws of Love?

MARY: To love God, yourself, and all people and creatures of the earth. From this all else will follow.

ANNA: Have you been appearing and/or speaking to so many people because you want to tell us how we can reach peace?

MARY: Yes, this is one of the main reasons. I want to help you all save yourselves and the world. You are all my children and all creations of God. And so I say again, pray for peace and tell others to do the same.

ANNA: The world is filled with people following different religions that teach different prayers. Should we say those prayers, too, or just talk to God?

MARY: You should do whatever feels right to you. When a Sufi recites his morning prayer "Praise be to Thee, Most Supreme God," the prayer is not only sacred but it is being said by other Sufis around the world which empowers the prayer and brings a unity between all those praying that prayer and God. It is right and good. The same is true of prayers in other religions. If those who recite the specific prayers of their religion feel a connection to the Divine through these prayers, then it is right and good.

ANNA: Can people say prayers of other religions and join in with all those saying the prayer?

MARY: Of course! What does it matter where the prayer originates as long as it speaks to your soul and your devotion to God? Any prayer whose words speak to your belief in God will connect you to him and raise your vibration. And, it is true that many prayers are similar as God's energy directs them to be. You may pray the prayers of the religion you ascribe to or you may pray the prayers of other religions or you may speak from your heart to God in your own words. Just pray.

ANNA: I can't help but ask, is there a perfect prayer?

MARY: As I have said, there is not one perfect way to pray. Pray in whatever way makes you feel connected to God. One way is not better than the other. Most important is that you pray. There are prayers from many religions whose words carry an energy and a vibration that is perfect, but also your own words as spoken from your heart are perfect. Jesus recited the prayer, and as it is written: "Our Father in heaven, hallowed be your name." He gave this prayer to all people. Like children you, too, come to God, by humbling and addressing him as Father and recognizing that he is the Father of all nations, the One who rules and loves us all. His name is sacred and honored by all people. "Your kingdom come, your will be done, on earth as it is in heaven." The world is longing for unity with God and to share paradise, the kingdom, with him. By doing the will of God and living a life that is right and good, this kingdom can be realized. And, my dearest, the kingdom is inside of each one of you. Search for it as the kingdom of God connects each one of you. "Give us this day our daily bread." This is a call to God to feed you with his love and to nourish you in his light so that you may live in accordance to his will. It is also a statement of faith that God will provide. ". . . and forgive us our debts as we forgive our debtors." The world is so filled with anger and resentment. You claim as you pray this prayer to forgive others, as you are forgiven. It brings you in line with the energy of God as it makes each one of you more like God. By forgiving as God does, you also can be forgiven. By doing so, you are raised to the highest level of love. Always forgive and live with an open heart to all people. As God recognizes your errant ways and forgives you, you are claiming to be like him as you recognize the same of others and forgive them. It is great to do so! "And lead us not into temptation, but deliver us from evil." People of the world are tempted by so many things. As this line is said, you are asking for protection against the Evil One. God will protect you and send legions of angels to be at your side to hold you up and make you strong against all that is not of God. Say this prayer and let the words fill you and your heart will fly. The words of this prayer can be said over and over and that is good and right. Yet, it was meant as an example of how to pray, how to honor God and to allow all goodness and love to enter your being. Go into your heart and pray in whatever way ignites your soul. If saying this prayer is right for you, then so be it. If not, pray in a way that is right and perfect for your whole being.

ANNA: St. Paul said we should pray "unceasingly." How can this be accomplished in our busy lives?

MARY: You must remember that prayer is also a state of being. It is not only verbal but active. If you are a good person acting in love and seeking union and peace with all people, then you are living in prayer. If you worship God above the things of the world, you are living in prayer. If you live in gratitude for the blessings bestowed upon you and acknowledge these favors of God, then you are living in prayer. Living in a way that respects and loves all of God's creation is a powerful connection to God and makes you more godlike. It is an active prayer. Simply saying "thank you, God" as you go about your days and nights, is a prayer. Saying to your child "I love you" is a prayer, for those simple words speak volumes. Recognize that you are a being of the light; born of the light of the world and when you shine in love, you are healing the world and yourselves. You become like a lighthouse beaconing the lost and lighting the way as you are filled with the spirit of God. People recognize the light that shines from your soul. You are bringing the world to a place that welcomes peace. Verbal prayer must be followed by active prayer or it is hollow and insubstantial. I implore you to pray and live in the goodness of the light.

ANNA: You mentioned previously there are other ways to pray, not just with set prayers from various religions. Sometimes I just don't have the words to express what I am feeling or just don't know how to give myself over to prayer. There are times when I am just too exhausted to really pray. How do I pray then?

MARY: Don't overthink, just relax and give yourself up to him and you will be filled with the highest love. Ask the angels and ask *me* to pray with you. Allow yourself to receive his abundant peace.

ANNA: I don't want to bother you . . .

MARY: Oh, my dearest, how can you, or any of my children, bother me? I am your mother, the energy that longs for you to call me so that I may help you and be with you! Never feel as though you are "bothering" anyone in the Divine realm. We are filled with joy when we are called to pray with you, help you with your life, and aid you in your yearning to be closer to God. It doesn't matter what you are praying for, it is the act of coming before God, humbling yourselves, that is most important. Call on me, talk to me, let me in! It is my greatest desire to be a part of your life and lead you to the great altar.

ANNA: Thank you, Mother. It is so wonderful to know that you are there for all of us. We spoke about praying in silence and with words, but many religions—Hinduism, Buddhism, Christianity, as well as certain branches of Islam—use chanting as a means of prayer. Is that another way to pray?

MARY: I love to hear the music of singing or chanting! And, the angels revel in the music and sing along with all who chant or sing. Your voices are instruments of Divinity and God is elated by the sounds. Chanting is not only musical but can change the vibration of the world by the beauty and purity of the sound. Often, it does not require language so that all people can sing praise to God in the vibration of the chant. Whether one is using a mantra or just an intoning sound, when its purpose is to connect to Divinity, it is as enchanting as a virtuoso moving her fingers and creating music from a violin. And by chanting, the vibration of the person chanting, as well as all those around that individual, is elevated to a higher state of consciousness. This is true of all prayer, but the beauty of chanting is that when there is no language and the heart speaks, your consciousness cannot judge the prayer. Your soul is able to sing through the vibration of sound and leave the conscious mind at rest. Remember that God has intelligence but is also an energy that vibrates. When you chant, the vibration is mingled with the vibration of the earth, the people of the earth, all of heaven, and with God.

ANNA: Are you saying that it is better not to think when we pray?

MARY: It depends. Sometimes thinking and speaking to God in your language is good and right; it is good to consciously connect and focus on God. Being able to verbalize and talk to God is good. Other times, it is important to let your soul speak through chanting or music. But it is important that you pray in whatever way is good and right for you. You don't have to commit to one way or another; you can be flexible. Be devoted to God and communicate in whatever way makes you feel his love. You were created to share your soul, your mind, and your being in various ways with God and so you must do so in a way that is right for you.

ANNA: Is there is a specific chant that is stronger than others?

MARY: All chants as well as all prayers that are intended to reach God are good and right. Yet, the intoning of *Om* is a perfect sound and is the sacred vibration of God. It vibrates with the earth, all creation, and heaven. The Hindus teach that, in the beginning, as the world was being formed, the vibration of the most holy one preceded language. In chanting *Om*, it is easier to go into the soul as thoughts are tuned out and the vibration of the sound overtakes the physical body. *Om* awakens the soul as well as the physical being. Yet, of most importance is the intention of the song or chant as a way to connect with God. Be sincere in your prayer whether it is a chant, oral prayer, thought, or silent prayer. One is not better than the other. All are good and perfect when you reach out to God with an open and sincere heart.

ANNA: So chanting is another form of meditating, a tool for reaching our soul! There is so much to understand! What about music? Are songs prayers?

MARY: Again and again I say "the angels adore music!" When you sing, the angels sing with you. Music that is made to bring joy, love, and unity is a prayer. I love it when you all sing together. Your hearts become lighter and the glory of God is revealed in the notes. God is so good; he created you to bring joy to yourselves and to him in so many ways. Keep it simple. There is no reason to complicate the gifts that were given to you. Praise him, pray with me and all people, pray alone, just follow your heart and let your prayers develop organically. You are all perfect beings of light, sound, and intelligence. Follow where your heart leads. And in music where there are no words, all can pray together. Music has no language and yet encompasses all languages. Sometimes the notes of the music can move your souls and bring you together with other people of all nations to raise your unified vibrations to the highest Power. There are places in the world where music is intentionally played to raise vibration and that prayer is welcomed in heaven.

ANNA: You have asked me to include meditations throughout this book. Is there a difference between meditating and praying?

MARY: In its purest sense, when meditation is used to leave the conscious mind and go into the soul with the purpose of reaching

God, it is a prayer. Meditation can be used for so many things, but at its core it is a connection to the soul as the mind is pushed away. As you go into your higher self, your soul, you can connect with heaven.

ANNA: What would you say to claims that going deep into the soul can open a person up to evil? There are also those who insist meditation belongs only to religions that teach it as part of their religion.

MARY: Oh, my child, this should all be so simple! Meditating and connecting with your soul and the Divine essence inside of you is perfect and right. It is a way to experience a form of bliss. If people protect themselves by calling on the power of God, there is nothing wrong or bad in that. This practice does not belong to one religion but to all people!

ANNA: I explained how to meditate in the beginning of this book. Yet, I didn't explain how to meditate unguided, nor how to incorporate it into prayer. Can you give us some guidelines to transform my unguided meditations as a way to connect to God?

MARY: Don't complicate meditation. Call in the power and presence of God. Pray in faith. Pray. Then as you finish praying, enter a state of silent prayer as you sit in the energy of your thoughts and words. Allow your breath to connect with the breath of God. Allow yourself to feel and hear if God chooses to speak to you. Ask me to be present. I will fill your vessel with love and help you to receive. You may feel and know messages from your soul. It is all good and right.

ANNA: Thank you, Mother. This is a wonderful and beautiful way to meditate and be with God. Should we also focus on scripture or the holy words of God as written in various holy texts?

MARY: If you so desire. It is your choice.

ANNA: Is guided meditation better than unguided meditation?

MARY: They both have their place. It is at the discretion of the individual. Each way moves the person to their soul.

ANNA: I have read that scientists have discovered that daily meditation can change the characteristics of one's mind for the better. This, naturally, makes me think about fate. Does God truly want us to be able to choose our own path in life? Is it okay to evolve as humans?

MARY: If God didn't want people to choose their own path in life humans would be no better than machines or robots. In your choices you show your love for him and each other. In your free will you can choose to be more like him. Your earthly existence is about learning, about choosing to be your truest self and an extension of God's love. Life is a great adventure and should be cherished.

Meditation for Chapter Three

+ Gently close your eyes and breathe. Ask the angels
  to surround you in a brilliant circle of light, love, and
  protection. Imagine a column of light from heaven
  moving into the crown of your head, spreading through
  your body, and anchoring you to the core of the earth.
  Feel this wonderful light moving through your spinal
  column up from the tips of your toes. Allow your body
  to relax as you focus on your breath. Be aware of the rise
  and fall of your chest as you breathe in all that is good

and right in the universe. Be aware that you are filling your lungs with the Divine breath of God. Imagine your breath as a gentle wave moving back and forth and back and forth. Feel your body relax after each exhale as you release stress, negativity, and all else that doesn't serve you. Be conscious of how wonderful this feels. It is truly a gift to permit relaxation and peace into your mind, body, and soul.

+ Allow the energy of Mary, of her love and peace, to enter your body with each inhale. Exhale all that doesn't serve you: all stress, anxiety, anger, animosity, self-recrimination, and anything else that might get in the way of connecting to heaven. As you move into that wonderful place of total relaxation, begin to feel a sensation of peace moving through your body. It feels wonderful. Bask in this peace and relax. As you continue to feel the rise and fall of your chest as you breathe, imagine there is a silky pale blue light encircling your body. You feel its gentle vibration as it swirls around you, alerting and filling your senses. Just allow yourself to be, as this blue vibration floats around you. Know that it is good. Let this vibration hug you gently. Recognize this vibration to be Mother Mary. Let her warm presence move your focus from your breath to the soft beating of your heart. Envision your heart becoming larger in your chest as you let her in. See the soft blue that is circling around you ease into your physical body and your heart. Imagine that your whole being is reaching out to her. As you allow the soft blue light to fill your heart, recognize that both you and

Mary are blending energetically; you are becoming one essence. Delight in knowing that you are vibrating with her energy. As you breathe, begin to feel her more and more and allow yourself to go deeper. Now imagine a clear space, free of thought, and allow your breath to wander in silence. Visualize Mary standing in front of you; whatever image that works best for you is fine. She can continue to be the pale blue light or a feeling, or perhaps you may want to personify her. Again whatever seems right or feels right.

✦ See her reaching out her hand or see her energy expanding toward you and hear her say, "Pray with me and I will pray with you." Reach out to her. You see her kneeling before you, you feel the velvety warmth of her hands as she touches your hands and then places her hand on your heart. She brings your hands together in the prayer position and does the same with hers. As she begins to pray, her aura, the luminous blue light, fills the room. You not only hear her as she prays, you feel the love that is radiating from her. You intone your own prayer. Mary shows you an image that is the answer to your prayer. She tells you to claim the answer in faith. Take the time to see and feel this answer manifesting in all of your senses. When you are ready, hear Mary say "Let us pray for all those who seek God and cannot find him. Let us pray for love and peace in the world. Let us pray that my words will be known and people will once again come to God on bended knee. Thank you, God." Pray with her. Know that you are being blessed by God.

4

Why Are We Here?

What Role Does Fate Play in Our Lives?

ANNA: Mother Mary, I often wonder about God's plan. Why did he create us?

MARY: So many people over the ages have pondered this question. The answer is so simple that it defies logic. He created you to share his love. In the beginning there was only Love. God is that Love. Yet love cannot exist alone. Love seeks another to unite with. It seeks a balance of giving and receiving. In the beginning this great energy of pure love, this God as we call it, needed others to share with him all that he was and still is. And so, this Love sought an extension of itself and began to create. God created the world but the world, with its seas, oceans, mountains, and plains, did not love the Creator back in a way that filled his heart and mind. God is an intelligent being. The Creator then designed the creatures of the world but they, too, although they loved, didn't love in a way that fulfilled the Creator. These creatures walked the earth and followed their instincts of love but they didn't have the intelligence to love at the highest level. The animals that roamed the earth, wandered by instinct to protect themselves and their species, to procreate and live on.

ANNA: Why would God, who is all love, who made us in the image of this Love, allow free will? Why do we have the ability to choose to love or not to love God?

MARY: My child, you so love your freedom as all people do! God wants to be loved by choice, not by demand. That is true love. The ability to choose elevates love to the highest degree. God gave all people intelligence and that intelligence motivates them to choose to either serve themselves or to serve God. True love is a choice and a deep desire to have a relationship with God. This love is the strongest and most powerful force in the universe. Without this choice to love or not to love, love becomes an involuntary action and is empty. Love is not empty; it encompasses all that is. And, when you choose to love God you are, in turn, choosing to love yourself. This love elevates your soul and makes you more fulfilled as a person and as a soul. Humans were granted a strong heart to be filled and to give love. Humans were given a soul that recognizes God, and a mind in which to reason.

ANNA: And so, we evolved from some of the species that walked the earth in the beginning of time. Are we so different at this point?

MARY: There are still similarities. Many are apparent. For instance, like the animals, humans still have the need to protect themselves and their young and also the attraction to another of the species to procreate. Yet, humans also have strong instinct not just for survival, but to desire that which is good and right and to be able to reject and protect themselves from what is wrong. That is one of the ways that the species is superior to the other creations. But it is the similarities and the connection back to creation that unify all living things in the world.

ANNA: Did God have other ideas for the world in allowing humans to emerge?

MARY: Although God wants people to look at love and life in a simple way, he is very complex. God also sought balance in the world. Once humans were created the world was in balance and God provided all that was necessary for survival. There was water and food to allow people to physically grow and be strong; intelligence to apply logic and reason; the sun to warm people and give them light; the moon to relax and bring darkness so that people could rest their bodies. And, most important, the ability to recognize the great Love in all that was in creation and beyond. God so loves when his people give thanks for the sun, the moon, the fish that swim in the lakes, and the birds that fly in the sky. And, he allows the human race to continue to evolve in all ways.

ANNA: Does God want us to worship the earth?

MARY: Only God is to be worshipped. Yet, the earth is to be honored and respected. Heaven cries each time a piece of creation is destroyed. People take for granted the perfection of the earth as they abuse it. Humankind has not shown reverence for this planet that has given them sustenance and life. The earth, with its mountains, sky, trees, oceans, and seas needs to be protected. The earth in all its glory never stops teaching. Look to nature to learn about birth, death, and rebirth. It is all there. The earth is born in the spring, nurtures beauty and the new life in the summer, purges in the autumn, dies in the winter only to be reborn again in the spring. It's all there and mirrors the life of human beings. God set it all in motion so that you may understand. I say don't destroy that which nourishes you, gives you strength, and teaches you. Look to the mountains and the streams for peace . . . See God and feel his power in all creation.

ANNA: You talk about evolution. Is God evolving?

MARY: I wish you could see me smile at your innocence. My daughter, people and creatures evolve; God is evolved. God didn't evolve as humankind did, he was always evolved. This is a difficult concept to understand by humankind since it defies logic and the way that science works. Just know this: God is the only one who can say "I Am." God is constant and always the same. People are constantly changing individually, culturally, and globally; sometimes becoming something different from what they were a minute before or centuries before. A person's emotions change throughout the day. God just is, he doesn't become. God is the spark, the flame, and the light, and always has been. Someday, you will understand.

ANNA: That gives me comfort to know that God is never changing and that he will love forever. So what of the other creatures that walk the earth. Does he love them any less because they cannot return love to him?

MARY: He loves all of his creations. The creatures of the earth are innocent. They act out of instinct and a need to survive. His love is so great and incomprehensible that there is no weighing who or what he loves more. Love is love. Don't seek to define God's love, just accept it and return it. All creatures of God are related and should be honored. God does not provide a contest with one person or group to win his love. He loves all. And he loves the land on which you build your lives. He loves the sky, the rain, and the snow. He loves it all. He is Love and created all out of this great love.

ANNA: But you said his plan was to create beings that he could love and who could love him. Did he make a mistake in creating the creatures? Why didn't he create man from the very beginning?

MARY: God doesn't make mistakes. Although he so desired to share love with his creation, he still wanted his creatures to crave him. And so God permitted the yearning for his love to emerge. As the creatures of the earth evolved from living by instinct and fighting for survival, they began to feel the need for something more. This yearning has carried on through the ages to all of you and will continue until all are with God in his kingdom. This yearning is part of each person as it grew from the creatures who were formed by God in the beginning.

ANNA: And so you say that this ancient yearning still exists inside each one of us?

MARY: Of course it does, my dear one. As you recognize God's love as a part of who you are, you will begin to want more. The more you know God, the more you will feel his love. As you feel his love, you will crave more as it will sustain you and bring you tremendous joy. As a creation of love, you will always seek to fill the void inside yourself with love. Yet, the greatest love, the preeminent love, is God. You will continue to yearn for that love until you are in the arms of God. What your mind does not understand, your soul does. Your soul longs to be in union with God's energy. Your soul longs for the love that only God can give. As the soul yearns, the heart aches for the love. Intellectually, this is difficult to understand, but it is so.

ANNA: Why do we have to wait? If God truly loves us and allowed this evolution so that we could love at the highest level, then why isn't God walking among us?

MARY: God is among you! God is inside you, each and every one of you. Each person is an extension of that love. This love inside each one of you is perfect; it is the very essence of God. It is what you want more of. God also gave me to all people so that I could lead people to him. I will take everyone to that Love if they listen with their hearts.

ANNA: But why can't we have heaven on earth?

MARY: That is a very insightful and merited question. The human race had the chance to live in paradise. The vibration of love did exist in the beginning and exists now. Although prophets, teachers, and others, through God's grace, have tried to make people understand the Truth of God, and to follow God, people have still turned from him, not wanting to hear his message. God's desire is to bring heaven to all of you, but people through the ages, in great numbers, have turned from him. They have taken the words from the prophets and turned them around to feed their greed and selfishness. The people of the earth need to hear him and then the world can be healed. Only then will there be one kingdom.

ANNA: Humans took the love of God and through free will really messed up this world. It makes me very sad and yearn for God all the more. Did you feel the yearning in your life?

MARY: The yearning, for me, to bask in the love of God, was like poetry. The pain of being separate made me live in the way I did; searching for union with God. This pain and the urge to be one with God allowed my faith to grow even when I was faced with condemnation. Over the centuries poets try to convey this desire. Just as there are no words to truly describe love, this desire to be in a union with love is lost in language.

ANNA: I guess we have all felt that we have been lost or wandering in the wilderness of life. But if we are all longing for this love, why is there hatred and anger in the world?

MARY: People have the ability to choose right or wrong. They have the ability to reject that part of themselves that is the light and move to the darkness, and sometimes they don't realize they are. Each person embodies both the light and dark. They deny the longing for God and try to replace it with the yearning for material things and means to fulfill their own power. The yearning is there, yet sometimes it is mangled when people adore the material things of the world above God.

ANNA: Why would God, who made us in the image of his Love, allow this to be? Why do we have the ability to choose to love or not to love God?

MARY: I understand that this is difficult for you to comprehend. God wants to be loved by choice, not by demand. That is true love. The ability to choose elevates love to the highest degree. God gave all people intelligence, and that intelligence motivates them to choose to either serve themselves or to serve God. True love is a choice and a deep desire to have a relationship with God. This love is the strongest and most powerful force in the universe. Without this choice to love or not to love, love becomes an involuntary action and is empty. Love is not empty; it encompasses all that is. And, when you choose to love God you are, in turn, choosing to love yourself. This love elevates your soul and makes you more fulfilled as a person and as a soul.

ANNA: So why doesn't God just fix us and this crazy world if he loves us so much?

MARY: As I mentioned above, evolution has not ceased and he gave us free will. He is waiting for the people to return to him of their own choice. God created a world that is forever evolving.

God created love—not fear, pain, and hate. Humans did that. Humans brought into being confusion and barriers between each other. God created the world to be an extension of his love but humans desired more. It wasn't enough to connect with the forest and the trees, to feel and be grateful for the warmth of the sun and praise the Lord under the stars. People wanted much more. The love inside was and is pushed aside for power and dominion. God is the ultimate power—there is no greater power—and yet nations kill to have dominance. You must pray for this to end. It will only bring more destruction and unrest. I weep tears of blood because of this pain and destruction that has been brought forth by the need for power. I am crying out to all people to pray and recognize that God is the power. I am praying for this to end and that peace and love will shine on all creatures of the earth.

ANNA: So the human race is destined to fail if this fight for supremacy continues? In the end, if one nation rules will that suffice?

MARY: The only nation that will rule in the end is the kingdom of God. No one will win this game of supremacy; God is the power, God is supreme.

ANNA: So if this fight for supremacy is a losing battle, is God just watching us to see what happens? Is life just one big game?

MARY: No! You are the essence of God. God wants people to choose to be one with each other as they are one with him. Part of finding and sustaining peace and love is in helping one another, even those who fight and seek supremacy. This is not a game, but it is a battle. A battle of love versus fear and hate. Pray for those who seek power that they may find the light. Pray that they may understand that they cannot find what they seek on the earth but rather with God in his kingdom. The more people who pray for peace, the quicker it will happen. Don't give up and ignore the power of God in answering this prayer. The love of God is stronger than anyone. It is with the armor of God that this battle can be won.

ANNA: I cannot accept this easily. As a mother, I want to save my children from pain. I try to do all that I can to stop them from hurting. If God is the ultimate parent, why isn't he trying to help us stop the suffering?

MARY: God has given each person a piece of himself. You are blessed with this piece and it provides you the ability to make the right choices. You are a parent, and you have learned that you cannot control your children. As a mother, I couldn't dictate the choices of my children; I could not stop Jesus from fulfilling his mission on earth. I couldn't stop him when he frightened and angered the Pharisees. I couldn't protect him from what he saw fit to do. He surrendered to God and followed his path. When people surrender to the will of God, they are led to the right path, but the choice is to follow or choose another way. God allowed temptation. He wanted the choice to follow him to be of great consequence and made out of the highest love. It isn't easy to give up the need for power. It is difficult for people to recognize and give themselves over to a greater power than themselves. It isn't easy to worship a God that you cannot see over the luxuries of life. Yet, God is helping humanity. He is opening doors for peace to follow. You must all walk through the doors. You must all spread the word that God is bringing peace. People must open their eyes and correct their ways so that it can happen.

ANNA: I worry that one person cannot control the hearts and minds of all people. What can we do, on an individual level, to influence others?

MARY: Pray, pray, pray. Go to the Father in prayer. Pray for peace and love among all people; all nations. Remember also, as I have said previously, prayer is also state of being. It is not only verbal but active. Pray in whatever way you can. Through prayer you will align with the essence of the Divine. Through prayer you will be filled with more compassion and love. You will begin to radiate this light and all will see. And remember, each person is important when it comes to changing the world and bringing Love in.

ANNA: Is it wrong to like the luxuries that money can buy? Is it wrong to want the material things of the world? Is it "worshipping the golden calf"?

MARY: It is not wrong to enjoy the luxuries of your life. It is not wrong to want things that bring you happiness. But things cannot be objects of true love. You may like your house but your home cannot share love with you, nor you with it. It is wrong to worship anything or anyone above God. Just remember the things of the world disappear, and in the end there will always be God. And, you may respect people, but only God is to be worshipped. There is only one God. In saying this, people who live in poor areas of the world should not be pitied. If they have food and can take care of their families, they may even feel rich. Many of these people are very close to heaven, as they seek God to give them what they need for a peaceful life. They don't understand the desire for things that fill the houses of the wealthy, because those things are not of their world. How fortunate are these people!

ANNA: Are you saying that we shouldn't try to help the poor?

MARY: I am trying to clarify and help you to understand that living simply, like those who don't have money to buy material things, can be a gift. It is more difficult for the poor in societies where wealth is known. It is difficult when there is knowledge of what money can bring. But for those who live in areas where the things that money can buy is unknown to them, there is no desire for things. Many of these people don't want to be changed. I know of being poor from my own life on earth. My family was poor in material things. But I was rich in spirit and my love of God. I didn't lust after the silks of the wealthy women around me, but I sought and rejoiced in the love of family and God. However, when we could buy a piece of pottery or a rug, we did so with gladness and I enjoyed the beauty of the things without worshipping them. You may own things, but God is not a thing to be owned. Only God is to be worshipped and glorified.

ANNA: Perhaps what you are saying is that we are to enjoy the luxuries but not get lost in them as a means to satisfy the craving in our souls for God. Is that right?

MARY: Yes, my daughter. You don't have to rid yourself of all the things that you have, just adore only God. Don't allow material things to replace your love for God. In your free will, recognize, love, and follow God. Sing the praises of God and treat all people with kindness, compassion, and respect. Remember, things will disappear; love will last forever.

ANNA: What if I adhere to all of this and worship God but follow the wrong religion?

MARY: If a religion is based on love and teaches love among all people, how can it be wrong?

Meditation for Chapter Four

+ Gently close your eyes and breathe. Ask the angels
  to surround you in a brilliant circle of light, love, and
  protection. Imagine a column of light from heaven
  moving into the crown of your head, spreading through
  your body and anchoring you to the core of the earth.
  Feel this wonderful light moving through your spinal
  column up from the tips of your toes. Allow your body
  to relax, as you focus on your breath. Be aware of the
  rise and fall of your chest as you breathe in all that
  is good and right in the universe. Be aware that you
  are filling your lungs with the divine breath of God.
  Imagine that your breath is a gentle wave moving back
  and forth and back and forth. Feel your body relax
  after each exhalation as you release stress, negativity,
  and all else that doesn't serve you. Be conscious of how
  wonderful this feels. It is truly a gift to permit relaxation
  and peace into your mind, body, and soul.

+ Allow the energy of Mary, of her love and peace, to
  enter your body with each inhale. Exhale all that
  doesn't serve you: all stress, anxiety, anger, animosity,
  self-recrimination, and anything else that might get
  in the way of connecting to heaven. As you move
  into that wonderful place of total relaxation, begin to
  feel a sensation of peace moving through your body.
  It feels wonderful. Bask in this peace and relax. As
  you continue to feel the rise and fall of your chest as
  you breathe, imagine there is a silky pale blue light
  encircling your body. You feel its gentle vibration as it

swirls around you, alerting and filling your senses. Just allow yourself to be, as this blue vibration floats around you. Know that it is good. Let this vibration hug you gently. Recognize this vibration to be Mother Mary. Let her warm presence move your focus from your breath to the soft beating of your heart.

✦ Envision your heart becoming larger in your chest as you let her in. See the soft blue that is circling around you ease into your physical body and your heart. Imagine that your whole being is reaching out to her to be a part of her. As you allow the soft blue light to fill your heart, recognize that both you and Mary are blending energetically; you are becoming one essence. Delight in knowing that you are vibrating with her energy. As you breathe, begin to feel her more and more and allow yourself to go deeper. Now imagine a clear space, free of thought, and allow your breath to wander in silence. Visualize Mary standing in front of you; whatever image that works best for you is fine. She can continue to be the pale blue light, or a feeling, or perhaps you may want to personify her. Again whatever seems right or feels right. See her reaching out her hand or see her energy expanding toward you.

✦ As you begin to feel her gently filling your senses, hear her say *I want to show you Love*. Imagine her reaching out to you with her energy. She lifts you up. You begin to fly through wispy clouds to a place filled with beautiful colors—vibrant majestic purple mountains, glistening blue streams, verdant green grass, and bright yellow and orange flowers blooming everywhere. Take in the colors of this magical place. Hear Mary ask, *Do you choose to be in the presence of Love?* Hear yourself saying yes and, just as you do, see everything around you become more brilliant. Your loved ones, who have passed from the earth, begin to fill the empty spaces with their presence. Perhaps they speak to you. Feel the love that is all around. It grows stronger and stronger. Take this time to listen. When you are ready, hear yourself saying *I accept love, as I accept and love my Creator above all. I choose to worship only one God.* Feel God's love streaming into your body as you relax in the purity of his presence.

5

The Power of Faith

*What Role Should Religion
Play in Our Lives?*

ANNA: You say no religion is wrong if it focuses on love, but there are so many religions these days. It seems that every religion believes their way is the only way. Is there one perfect religion among them all?

MARY: My dear, there is no "perfect" anything made by humans. Only God is perfect. Any religion that focuses on sharing love and peace is good but there is no "one perfect religion." Humankind has been searching for the Truth for so many centuries. People have been seeking an explanation for all that exists. In their quest, questions have increased. Religion is man-made, a way to gather and build a community of people who share the same faith and beliefs. It is comforting to share a common belief. That is good and right. Still, God created you ALL. God did not pick and choose any one religion. In the beginning there was only God. No religion was necessary.

ANNA: Can there be many right religions?

MARY: Yes, there are many ways to adore and worship God. Religion doesn't bring you to God, living in a way that is good and right according to God brings you closer to him. God does not judge where you find the way and the Truth; it is only important that you recognize that you are a being of love and your purpose is to share Love. There are many religions that can bring you to this truth.

ANNA: Is religion the only way to find God?

MARY: There are so many people who walk the earth! They are all different and will find God in so many ways and in so many places! It is wonderful! Of course people can find God in religion or outside of religion. Religion can be a negative force when it promotes the creation of fear; a fear of those who are not like you or who threaten your identity. The chosen are not few. The chosen don't fill one church or temple and not another. The chosen are all people. How people decide to live is based upon their own free will. There is no ideal place to worship God. A religion should be welcoming of all people, for all people were created by God. All people belong to God, not just one group.

ANNA: Is this another one of the reasons you are coming to us now? Is it important for people to know this?

MARY: Yes, this is one of the primary reasons I am now here. I am also here to show all the way. I am with you all to unveil the Truth to those who are lost in religion and dogma. I want to divert all that do not speak of love and about the Creator. I am here to teach you how to take down the barriers that hold you apart and create wars and suffering. I am here to guide the world to peace. But people must change their way of thinking.

The world must accept a union of all people as children of one God without prejudice and without pride. It is only then that the battle for supremacy between nations and people will be lost. It is only in understanding and accepting each other's differences that the world will be saved. I am praying for unification and acceptance across religions and for all people to truly know that each and every one of them carries the energy and vibration of God. All are the same and all people are one in that Love. It must be accepted for peace to reign. I ask you all to pray with me for this to happen.

ANNA: Through the years people have been killed in the name of religion. Crusades and wars have been fought with the banner of God flying. Today the world is suffering at the hand of terrorism. ISIS declares that their acts of violence and terrorism are consistent with their religion and God. What are we to think about this?

MARY: Oh, my daughter, the pain of these actions rips through my heart. ISIS, or any other group that kills in the name of God, is not following him and is not a religion that is based on Love or honored by God. ISIS commands the opposite of love as it has brought great fear to people. Anything that comes from God is love and connects and builds unity among his people. My tears are flowing from the destruction these groups have caused. Any killing in the name of God does not and never did come from God and is a travesty of all that is good in the world. People have used religion to cloak their real motivation of supremacy and power. This must stop! Only God is supreme! As my tears flow, I am lifting up all people of the world to be cleansed in the energy of Love. All people should pray constantly for the cessation of these acts of terrorism. Ultimately love will prevail. Pray that the barriers between people fall. Pray, pray, pray. It can be.

ANNA: Okay then, different issue, but since we're on the subject of balance and tolerance in religion, there has been controversy over whether or not is it moral for two women or two men to be married and have a family. Is it moral?

MARY: If there is love between two people and they are in line with what is good in the world, and follow God, then it is right. God does not oppose. They can be a family. If they bring children into the unit, that is also a family.

ANNA: So homosexuality is approved by God? Even if some religions say it is not?

MARY: God is not judging the sexual desires of people. If two people love each other, so be it.

ANNA: You talk of barriers coming down and religions coming together in love. I'm not sure religion in our current world can achieve this. Should we, then, strive to do away with all religion?

MARY: Maybe someday there will be no religion on earth but that time is not here. Now, more than ever, people are seeking comfort from their religions. It is reassuring for people to know that God is providing love to them amid the destruction and pain they see in the world. And so, for the time being, religion can and does serve a purpose when it is for the glory of God and not man. When the purpose is to bring through the Truth and the Love that is God into the hearts of people, it is a good thing. And many religions can coexist if they promote love for all people. There is no religion in the kingdom of God. All are one and all are welcome if they have followed Love in their lives.

ANNA: Do you consider yourself a Jew or a Christian?

THE POWER OF FAITH

MARY: I was born into a Jewish family and raised my own family following the Jewish practices that I was taught. Among other things, I and my family held holy the Sabbath, celebrated the highest holy days, and ate clean meat. My religion taught me an obedience to God and faith. But, again, religion is of the earth not of heaven. I am of no religion and all religions. I wrap my mantle around all people. I ask that all people come to me for help and counsel. I belong to the world, not a certain religion. Remember, my son did not promote religion. He was astute in the Torah and showed obedience to the written law. He was a Jewish man living in a place of oppression. His words were not Jewish or Christian. His words were the words of the Father. His words spoke of love and peace and unity. He didn't come to the world to start a religion, rather he came to start a movement of love and to let people know of God. He loved both those that were treated cruelly and rejected by the masses, as well as the masses. He lived and died; he believed dying was necessary to bring us to God and to have the world live as God intended. His words became his legacy and his Truth. His words were and are the Truth of God. And so it was then and is now.

ANNA: I understand. There are many sacred books about God used by various religions. Are these books true?

MARY: If the book speaks of love and compassion it is true.

ANNA: The Old Testament has so many stories of wars and violence and depicts God as a being to be feared. I find this confusing since in the New Testament Jesus speaks of a God who is compassionate. Which one shows us the real God?

MARY: This question is one that so many have wondered about. People must understand that all the holy books and the Bible were written by men. These men, although inspired by God, interpreted God based upon their own cultures and their own view of life. So people must have an open mind when reading the holy books. The Bible is considered a historical account and it is also filled with teachings and the wisdom of God.

ANNA: The world right now is filled with evil atrocities. Are we doomed? Will God wipe us out, like he did in the story of Noah?

MARY: Oh, my daughter, you speak in fear! Don't ever let fear overtake your love and faith. Those who pray and stand in love must continue to pray. They will be saved. Don't only pray for yourself but for all people. You must pray for your enemies as well as for those who are close to your heart. Remember God created a means for his people to be saved when Noah created the Ark. It was the free will of the people to choose to be saved. It is the same today. I call to all people to choose to be saved.

ANNA: Sometimes being human can be so difficult. I try not to fear.

MARY: My daughter, I am here to take away your fear and replace it with love for all people of all religions.

ANNA: It seems to me that fear keeps us in our places and can be a controlling force. Consistent with the Old Testament, does God implant fear inside of us so that he can rule us better, perhaps keep us in line?

MARY: No! God doesn't want to control people with fear. God wants to bring joy into the hearts of his children. God does not want to rule as a king; rather God wants to be in partnership with those he has created. Fear is created out of a lack of faith and the absence of love. If you embody love and you have faith that God is around you and in you, there can be no fear. God's gift to you is unconditional love. That love has no boundaries and, in return, it brings peace. Since you live in a world where the actions of others affect you, your inner peace is influenced by all the energies of people in the world. Yet, within yourself, you can feel the peace that love brings and not be overcome by fear. And when you truly live in communion with God, you can have faith. Faith and love are the opposite of fear. Fear restricts love. Fear clouds the mind and senses and moves one from love. Fear is a product of the world and may act as a defense mechanism creating anxiety and worry. Of course, there is the real fear of putting your hand in a fire. But, I tell you this, even real fear can be fought with God. God will make it so that you can put your hand in the fire if your heart and soul are freely given to him.

ANNA: Since I'm still working on my faith I don't think I'll try that! But let me get this straight: If we have love there should be no reason for fear. Yet, for many, God is a fierce God who punishes people who are opposed to him.

MARY: God intervenes to show people the correct path. God is not an energy of wrath and punishment. Also remember, as I said earlier, the accounts of God in written texts rely on the accuracy of that author and societal beliefs and norms of those times. At the time of the writing of the Old Testament, the stories were based on a history of war, and the storytellers were seeking to make sense of the atrocities in their lives. These storytellers didn't focus on forgiveness but on learning by punishment. They were also seeking to instill the morality of God in the minds of the people. People understand right and wrong, reward and punishment. The way in which they wrote the Bible made sense. They established law and order in this way and introduced their people to God as well as setting forth rules for their society and culture.

ANNA: So God doesn't become angry with the flawed ways of the world, or any of us?

MARY: *Anger* is not the right word . . . God becomes disappointed. God can be hurt by his children. God is hurt by each and every person who sets out to destroy all that he made in Love. God is hurt by each and every person who turns from the good to that which is against him and his intentions for all his people.

ANNA: How are we to make sense of famines, diseases, and the devastation that sometimes come from nature? Is this God's work? Or is this just random turmoil?

MARY: God does not destroy; humans, by their free will, may destroy. All these horrible things that you mention were created, in some way, by humans. And, one person or one group may affect the whole world by its actions.

ANNA: Even natural disasters, like earthquakes?

MARY: Although the earth itself doesn't have intelligence, it has a vibration. When the earth is "disrespected" and its resources not honored, an imbalance is produced. When the earth is not in balance, natural disasters occur in an attempt to bring back the balance.

ANNA: I never looked at it that way before . . . but what about progress? Our advances in medicine, our scientists studying global warming? What does God think of all this?

MARY: People have been gifted by God with tremendous intelligence that can bring forth new things that may help people live their lives better and happier. The advances in medicine are good and right. Of course it is not good to create things that can hurt and destroy such as weapons of mass destruction.

The goal should always be to somehow help, love, and heal. Love others, respect the earth and all creatures that are a part of the world.

ANNA: I understand . . . You say you come for all religions, what if members of other religions either don't know you or don't identify with you?

MARY: I have come in the past in many different forms to many different people. For those who don't know me, this is my way of introducing myself as the mother of humanity. Once again, I say, I am here for all people. And for those who don't identify with me, that is okay, too. Again, you have free will.

ANNA: So like God you are here for all people regardless of their religions?

MARY: Yes, I am an extension of God's love and am here for all, as is God.

ANNA: What of religions that worship many gods?

MARY: There is only one God. Yet, many of these religions have one main God and many inferior gods. These other gods are similar to the prophets and saints in other religions. These religions are not to be judged as immoral based upon their hierarchy. If God is at the top of the hierarchy and reigns supreme, the religion is in line with the desires of God. The Hindus adore Shiva, Vishnu, and Brahma, which are really just different names and personalities of one God. They are similar to the Christian trinity. Do not judge other religions that promote Love. Look within yourself and what practices you are following. Share God's love. Speak of God's love, and more and more people will be brought to him and you will be blessed.

ANNA: I am wondering now about spirit guides. I have heard this term used many times. Can you tell me who they are and does each person have their own spirit guide? Do we have more than one?

MARY: Yes, my daughter, each person has at least one spirit guide in attendance around them at all times. Unlike the angels, spirit guides were human and passed on to the Divine realm. These wonderful spirits choose to help those on earth, especially those whom they love. Since they have been human they understand the trials, tribulations, and pain of being human as well as the joy. Again, since they are human spirits they are very easy to communicate with. My children, let them in to help you and lead you to God in all his glory. Let them bring you the healing you so seek!

ANNA: Do people have one particular guide that helps them in life?

MARY: People have many guides. Similar to guardian angels, spirit guides choose a specific person to "take care of." Again, people are never alone. People usually have many guides in addition to their guardian angel. You must consciously connect to the angels and your guides and allow them in to help you and guide you in life.

ANNA: How can we allow them in if we don't see them?

MARY: It is in feeling and listening to the voice in your head. Sometimes you know it is not your own voice. Don't discount this voice. It is an awakening! Open your eyes and ears to all that is on the other side of your normal vision. See with your heart . . . feel and listen in the silence. Pray and meditate in order to open up all of your senses to the "unseen" world around you.

ANNA: Can we talk about the saints and prophets for a moment? Did they all deserve such status?

MARY: Oh, my dear, you desire so much to know the Truth! You are all saints and prophets as you are all children of the Most High! Know that there is no one person whom God loves more than the next. All are equal. The world is God's church and you are all a part of it. A true saint or prophet is anyone who, in pure faith, opens their hearts to God and to his gifts. These people were and are of Love and carry no fear. All people now must follow their hearts in discerning what and who is teaching in accordance with God. You will know. Connect in prayer to the energy of God and feel the vibration in your soul. You will know the Truth. I will help you.

ANNA: You have said that the world is a church. Can you expand on that?

MARY: Churches, temples, and other houses of worship are structures within the world. They were erected as the place where people believe that God resides and people can come to worship him. And it is true, God does exist in these structures and as people pray in unity in these places, his vibration becomes stronger and stronger there. Yet, it must be known that God doesn't exist solely within these houses of worship. Look around you at all times and know that the earth is a church and its people clergy. Go outside into nature and see the magnificence of God in the plants and animals. Feel God's healing in the sun's brilliant rays and in the beams of light from the moon. God created the world to be a sacred place and so it is. Honor the earth and stop all the destruction of the holy ground on which you all walk. Give homage to the trees and lie in the grass and let heaven surround you. Many churches are filled with gold and jewels to show that God's house is a kingdom of richness. That is not necessary. The richness of God is in nature and all that he created. It is so simple and so right. Give honor where honor is due. Go to your houses of worship and pray in community with others but know that sacred ground and the house of God is all around you as you live your life in the world that Love created.

ANNA: You say that religions that worship God are good. What of Buddhism which does not recognize God but promotes compassion and love in the world?

MARY: There are many different traditions of Buddhism and the Buddhist beliefs regarding God vary. There is also the philosophy of Buddhism that has been adopted by people of many different religions. The Buddha was a teacher who taught empathy and awakened people to the energy of love inside themselves. That energy is God even without the recognition. Buddhism promotes compassion, peace, and love, which is consistent with the desires of God. Remember that religion is based upon man's culture and experiences. Buddhism was born out of Siddhartha Gautama's experiences and view of the world. His enlightenment took a form that resonated with these experiences.

ANNA: What about women and their place in religion? Can you talk to me about that?

MARY: The Bible speaks of strong women: Ruth, Esther, Elizabeth (my dear cousin), Sarah, and Hagar. Yet, each of these women was the catalyst for the men to do their work. Again, the holy books were written by men in a culture that didn't recognize women as their equal. That doesn't mean that women didn't have their place in spreading the Truth of God. It just wasn't always written as so. Mary from Magdala was as strong as any of the Apostles in her love for Jesus. She was also loved as much by Jesus as he loved the men that followed him. She spread his word and continued his work after his death.

ANNA: Does God have a gender?

MARY: God has no gender. He is neither male nor female and yet is both. He is a vibration that doesn't possess the physical attributes of a gender yet he possesses the emotional attributes of both. God is both the ultimate he and she.

ANNA: Does God have a color?

MARY: God does not have a "race." He is the highest vibration and carries all color.

ANNA: I must ask; do you have a preferred religion?

MARY: As I have said, if a religion is focused on Love and showing compassion to others and oneself it is good and right. I don't prefer one over the other. God is here for all people as I am.

ANNA: So many people, especially in the United States, are not a part of an organized religion. Is it okay to just be spiritual without joining a religion?

MARY: God did not start religion, people did. If people believe that God is Love and truly extend themselves to others without judgment and in peace, that is their religion. It is not necessary to join a group but proclaim God in your heart and share that Love with others! How perfect if all people did this no matter what religion or spirituality they practiced.

ANNA: All organized religion talks of some kind of afterlife. Does it exist?

MARY: Of course. You live to die and be born again in the kingdom of God.

Meditation for Chapter Five

✦ Gently close your eyes and breathe. Ask the angels
to surround you in a brilliant circle of light, love, and
protection. Imagine a column of light from heaven
moving into the crown of your head, spreading through
your body, and anchoring you to the core of the earth.
Feel this wonderful light moving through your spinal
column up from the tips of your toes. Allow your body
to relax, as you focus on your breath. Be aware of the
rise and fall of your chest as you breathe in all that
is good and right in the universe. Be aware that you
are filling your lungs with the Divine breath of God.
Imagine your breath as a gentle wave moving back and
forth and back and forth. Feel your body relax after each
exhale as you release stress, negativity, and all else that
doesn't serve you. Be conscious of how wonderful this
feels. It is truly a gift to permit relaxation and peace into
your mind, body, and soul.

✦ Allow the energy of Mary, of her love and peace, to
enter your body with each inhale. Exhale all that
doesn't serve you: all stress, anxiety, anger, animosity,
self-recrimination, and anything else that might get
in the way of connecting to heaven. As you move
into that wonderful place of total relaxation, begin to
feel a sensation of peace moving through your body.
It feels wonderful. Bask in this peace and relax. As
you continue to feel the rise and fall of your chest as
you breathe, imagine there is a silky pale blue light
encircling your body. You feel its gentle vibration as it

swirls around you, alerting and filling your senses. Just
allow yourself to be, as this blue vibration floats around
you. Know that it is good. Let this vibration hug you
gently. Recognize this vibration to be Mother Mary. Let
her warm presence move your focus from your breath to
the soft beating of your heart.

+ Envision your heart becoming larger in your chest as
you let her in. See the soft blue that is circling around
you ease into your physical body and your heart.
Imagine that your whole being is reaching out to her
to be a part of her. As you allow the soft blue light to
fill your heart, recognize that both you and Mary are
blending energetically; you are becoming one essence.
Delight in knowing that you are vibrating with her
energy. As you breathe, begin to feel her more and
more and allow yourself to go deeper. Now imagine a
clear space, free of thought, and allow your breath to
wander in silence. Visualize Mary standing in front of
you; whatever image that works best for you is fine. She
can continue to be the pale blue light or a feeling, or
perhaps you may want to personify her. Again whatever
seems right or feels right. See her reaching out her
hand or see her energy expanding toward you. She says,
"You are one with the universe. You are one with all
people. Come with me and we will find peace among
humanity."

+ Take her hand and let her lead you to an open field. You
walk on the lush green grass and see a circle of people
of all races, religions, ethnicities, and walks of life. You
take the hand of a person of another culture and feel

harmony as the energy of peace and love flows through
you. You allow all the judgment and prejudice that
you harbor in your body to leave. Imagine this energy
leaving you. Take your time. When you are ready,
feel a sense of freedom; you have released that which
separates you from other people. You now experience a
love that is flowing around the circle, moving through
your hands and connecting to your heart. It's as though
everyone's heart is connected by one piece of thread.
See these people, know that this circle is the fabric of
the universe. You no longer see the differences between
the people, but rather the similarities. You hear
laughter, one language, sense one face, and one heart.
Hear Mary say, "Love yourself and love one another
and you will be one with God, and he will be pleased."
Know that this is the first step toward acceptance and
universal love. Feel the blessings of heaven.

6

What Happens When We Die?

What Is Heaven?
Does Reincarnation Exist?

ANNA: Mother Mary, you say the kingdom exists inside of each one of us. Yet, you also say there is a heaven. Can you explain?

MARY: It is with great pleasure that I make this known to you and all people. It is important to know the answer and to make logical sense of it. The kingdom of God, as it exists in your soul, is the goodness of God and all his righteousness. It is this energy of Love that makes its home in your soul, along with the power of the Most High, God. He shares this with your soul so that you may know that God is always with you and in you. In its residency, it creates an innate intimacy and connection to God. That is the kingdom of God which resides inside of you. Yet heaven is outside of your soul and your physical being. It is a place the soul longs to rest in. Within heaven is the kingdom of God. Within heaven is the goodness of God, his righteousness, his Love, authority, and power. Do you understand?

ANNA: You have said to keep the concepts simple and so I am trying. So, the kingdom of God exists in all of us as a piece of God and keeps us connected to God. All that this is, all that it stands for, the very energy that it is, is also part of heaven. Is that correct?

MARY: And so you do understand!

ANNA: Mother Mary, talk to me of heaven. When I die will I be with you?

MARY: Yes, my sweet child, I will be waiting for you as I will be there for all my children.

ANNA: Mother, knowing that you will be there makes me so happy. Will I also be with my loved ones who have passed?

MARY: You will see and be with all whom you have loved during your life. Love is the connection that will bring you to those you cherished on earth. Love transcends all and never releases those whom it brings together. Love is the greatest gift that God has given to the world.

ANNA: I am wondering if those in heaven are not in their human bodies, will I be able to recognize the people who have passed before me?

MARY: You will recognize them by their unique energies and by their love. They will shower you with affection and introduce you to your ancestors.

ANNA: Can our loved ones, who have passed, present themselves in human form in heaven or only in the form of energy?

MARY: There is no need for anyone to see what the physical body looked like on earth after it has passed on. As you all go about your lives, you may not be aware of it, but you are sensing and actually seeing each other's energy. When you pass on and join your loved ones in the Divine realm, you will remember and recognize them by their individual energies.

ANNA: What if some of my ancestors were not nice people? Will they welcome me as well? Will they be in heaven?

MARY: If they have not reincarnated and have been through a life review and cleansing, yes, they will be there for you to meet.

ANNA: Does that mean the soul forgets its life on earth?

MARY: It is just purified in order to see its life with eyes of pure love and understanding. This is of utmost importance for its life review.

ANNA: What is a life review? Do we all have to go through that?

MARY: Life is not trivial; all lives have substance. Upon entering the Divine realm all must go through a life review. All must see the actions, inactions, the good and the bad things that they initiated and participated in during their lives. All must see and feel the love and happiness that they gave and received as well as the hate, anger, and pain given to others. And so, if someone intended harm to others, or created suffering in any form, then upon entering the realm of God, he or she must view the hurt and pain inflicted upon others. Since all are in their pure soul energy when in heaven, this causes great suffering and separation from God. The soul's one desire is to fulfill the will of God. This is where the term *hell* comes from. Hell is not the burning of the flesh that is depicted in paintings and literature. Hell is the chasm, the energetic barrier that keeps an impure soul from God. How can the soul burn when it is an energy that has no physical form? Hell is the fire burning in an impure soul, which is worse than the burning of the flesh. It is an intense pain that requires reliving all the suffering in any form that was caused by the soul to others on earth. This is torture. Yet God is a loving Father and once the review is completed the soul is given a chance to learn and be forgiven.

ANNA: So that is what Matthew was referring to when he said "while the sons of the kingdom will be thrown into the outer darkness. In that place there will be weeping and gnashing of teeth" (Matthew 8:12). It sounds so horrible!

MARY: It is most horrible for there is nothing worse! What is more abhorrent than going against the will of God and causing a separation from God? Hell is darkness; there is no light, it is a state of utter loneliness, where the soul burns in desperation for God. Yet, as I said, God is a force of love and love forgives those who seek forgiveness. But know forgiveness comes after the offender is forced into this place of "hell." One cannot be evil and easily get into the realm of God. Those going through this hell must be contrite and humble themselves as they seek forgiveness for their wrongdoings. They must come to terms with the reason for their transgressions and seek to repair their souls.

ANNA: How can we, as individuals, serve humanity in our current divisive climate?

MARY: The world was created to be a place of magnificence and peace among all creation. Right now is a very trying time all over the globe. Remember, in prayer all is possible. Pray for your leaders in government. Pray for the innocents and those who are seeking peace to make its way in. Pray for evil to be at bay. With prayer you and your leaders will find answers.

ANNA: It is so difficult to forgive other people when they hurt us. If someone does something intentionally to hurt another person, should they be forgiven by that victim?

MARY: You are all in the energy of God and must find it in your hearts to forgive. When you hold on to feelings of not forgiving others, you block yourselves from the love around you. This feeling pulls you from God. My child, show the world that God resides in you! Behave in a way that is godlike and others will follow.

ANNA: That can be very difficult. In forgiving, does that mean we have to stay in a relationship with people who hurt us?

MARY: If you choose to stay away from someone who has hurt you but pray for him or her, that is good. People cannot be forced to forget. It is sometimes right to stay away.

ANNA: I guess that is something so many need to learn to do. Many people say that earth is a classroom. Is this the place where we are supposed to learn?

MARY: Earth is indeed a classroom, a place to learn to be closer to and to unite with God. Those souls who have lived·in opposition to the Truth must return to earth to learn what they didn't learn; why they lived against God. This is their penance . . . to leave the realm of pure Love and return to human form. They are then given the chance to act more like creations of Love.

ANNA: I believe you are talking about reincarnation . . . Do only those who have done horrific deeds reincarnate?

MARY: You, my dear, are an old soul! No one is perfect on the earth. There are some who follow God more closely and are more enlightened, but not perfect. Only God in his majesty is perfect. But God made you all to strive for perfection and to love perfectly. That is what the soul desires. So, souls choose to come back to the earth to become "better" and more loving. They also come back to teach others about love and to heal the planet and its people. So not only those who have committed horrible deeds on earth reincarnate.

ANNA: It sounds to me like earth is more of a purgatory. Is that true?

MARY: It is . . . yet purgatory is just a name given to a state of being. It isn't a place but a state of yearning for Love and God. Souls exist in purgatory to learn and are given another chance to be "better." But the state of being of purgatory leaves the soul wanting God and his realm. The separation can be painful and lonely even when people are surrounded with other people. It is the conflict in the human condition. Humans strive for all on earth yet will not achieve true joy and happiness being so far from God. That doesn't mean that happiness is elusive. People can be happy, but true satisfaction, love, and joy can only be felt in union with God.

ANNA: The mystics of all different religions have spoken of reaching an ecstatic state where their souls are merged in intimate union with the Divine. They have said that when in this state they experience true joy. It sounds like they are entering a place that is heaven. Can you tell me more about that? Can we all reach this place while we are on earth?

MARY: Yes, all can reach this state. It is a grace bestowed on those who are devoted in mind, body, and spirit to God. And it is so that this state also has been experienced by those who practice different religions. God, in his perfect wisdom, allows all to come to him through this state of ecstasy. It is his way of showing the world that all can delight in him regardless of the religions that they practice. As many of the mystics have conveyed, there are many layers of reality, and much to be shed as one is made privy to the highest realm. This has been spoken of in languages of Hebrew, Greek, Coptic, Syriac, Arabic, Persian, Hindi, as well as the modern languages. People have been experiencing mysticism since the beginning of humankind.

ANNA: Many people these days have said that they have died and gone to heaven and then returned back to their own physical bodies. These "near death experiences" have even been reported by doctors who confirm it after speaking with their patients. And recently there have been doctors who have said that they have had their own near death experience and are bringing forward proof of it. Although scientists have many theories to disprove it, the stories continue to propagate. Are near death experiences true?

MARY: Yes, people may die temporarily and enter the realm of heaven but come back to their physical bodies and the earth. At this time in the history and evolution of humanity, there is a need to see and validate heaven. So many people are skeptics or don't believe in heaven or the realm of God. Thus, God in his glory has allowed people to glimpse a piece of heaven. These experiences are true.

ANNA: Many of these people who have experienced near death experiences report that they didn't want to come back. Why do they have to come back?

MARY: It is so that after being in the heavenly realm, even for a moment, it is difficult to desire to be anywhere else. Once there is a glimpse of heaven there will also be a yearning for it. It is painful to return to the body. Yet, some of these people are brought back to describe and give credence to their journey and spread the word or to change their lives or simply to complete their mission or soul purpose on the earth. In all cases, it isn't time to stay in heaven.

ANNA: I mentioned that recently there have been doctors and those in the medical profession who have reported to the media or written books about their own near death experiences. Are these stories true?

MARY: These stories are true and God and all in heaven are rejoicing. These men and women of science are bravely telling the world about their encounters in heaven. God in his infinite wisdom is allowing this brief viewing of heaven to be experienced by the skeptics and those in professions that can in some way validate these experiences. What is more believable than a person of science, a doctor, speaking about seeing heaven! You live in a society that honors education and those who hold positions of knowledge. Therefore, when a doctor claims to have seen heaven, people respect and accept the stories of their experiences in heaven. And their experience is validated by virtue of their position in society and the word is spread. God is blessing each one of these people who are speaking out about their "near death experiences." They are doing so as many in their professions mock them. It is the way . . . Many times the Truth is not understood initially but instead ridiculed. It was the same with Jesus.

ANNA: Can people also "glimpse" heaven in dreams?

MARY: When the body is resting, heaven can be viewed. The body rests while the soul is still awake. Many messages from the soul and the spirit world come through during dreams.

ANNA: I want to know more about heaven. Is it a place? Do you live there?

MARY: I delight in describing the realm of God. Language is lacking and insufficient in describing its grandeur! It is a state of pure love; a place where the human emotions that are not of Love don't exist. So there is no hate, fear, anger, loneliness, or despair. Heaven is a place of peace filled with the energy of God; of Love and the souls basking in the light of this love. I have my place in God's realm. I am close to the energy of him that is the great "I Am." I am blessed to be one who shares his energy and brings it to people on earth as I bring his messages to them as well. It is so difficult to comprehend the beauty of heaven. It is beyond what the imagination can conjure. Heaven is a place where it is not just sight that you experience. There is a feeling of unconditional love that is overwhelming. It is a state of being. It is a place and state of pure bliss. Can you understand?

ANNA: I am trying but am struggling. A place of being? I don't think I can wrap my head around that. Please help me understand.

MARY: It is a simple place of just being, nothing to want or desire because heaven is the place of the "All," the place of God and abundant love, where the soul revels in bliss. Do you understand?

ANNA: I think I do. It sounds so wonderful. I have heard that heaven is very close to all of us and separated from the earth by a veil. Is this true?

MARY: People so seek to visualize! They want to see and conjure images so as to make valid what they don't see with their eyes. I understand, I was once of the world. There is no actual "veil." You may imagine a thin veil separating the earth from heaven. This veil is close to you. You are in one dimension of reality while the veil separates you from heaven, which is in another dimension. This veil, like the veil that some brides wear, is hiding the beauty behind it. Once the veil is lifted an undeniable feeling of love pours out and amazing beauty is revealed. How beautiful is heaven! When the veil is lifted not only will you experience the arresting loveliness of the realm of God but you will be with your beloved, God. How wonderful this is!

ANNA: I am enthralled by your explanation; it is so poignant. Can you tell me more of heaven? You didn't mention music and angels playing trumpets, is that all made up?

MARY: Poets and artists have depicted heaven in such a way. God works through art, yet sometimes it is the symbolism, or what the art represents. Heaven is filled with all that is good and right. Many hear the angels singing in glory to God and instruments playing music that words cannot convey. Others see and feel other things. What is most important is that heaven is the place of Love. God is glorified by all in his realm.

ANNA: As a medium, when spirits come to me to speak with their loved ones on earth, they show me that they are engaged in activities that they enjoyed while living on earth. Is this true?

MARY: They show you this so that you can convey something that their loved ones can understand and recognize. Yet, sometimes in the heavenly realm souls continue to get tremendous joy out of the things that they did on earth. There is no limit to joy in heaven.

ANNA: Do those in heaven engage in activities?

MARY: The soul is always active and always moving. The activities of heaven are different than those on earth. Again, heaven is a state of being and just being and basking in the love of God. The soul lives to glorify God and share this love with others in the realm and on earth. Yet, also in heaven souls communicate and learn from each other. They may even enter a place like a school to learn the things that they didn't learn on earth. They may manifest things that they liked to do on earth and engage in similar activities. To give you a simple example, if a soul enjoyed dancing, that soul may find a musical band of other souls or they may manifest their favorite music to dance to. They are free to enjoy all that is good and right and brings them joy. They also prepare for the reincarnation but access what they need to learn when they enter the earth again. The souls in heaven visit their loved ones on earth to help them and guide them through visitation in dreams and other messages sent. Because they are energetic beings, they can move objects, direct music, and turn on lights and other energy-driven devices. They also rest in God's overabundance of love. It is difficult for you to understand how this can be wonderful, but it is. You are all so focused on your lives and caught up in "living" that it may be difficult to conceptualize how this can be the ultimate happiness. Yet, there is no joy compared to being in the Divine realm.

ANNA: That explanation makes sense to me. What of animals? I love my animals . . . Will they find a place in heaven?

MARY: Animals are creatures of God and fill heaven. Dogs and other domesticated animals love with a purity that brings happiness to people and to God. Yes, animals exist in the realm of God. They may not have the capability to speak of their love, but it is a different form of love that cannot be denied.

ANNA: So many people have a fear of dying. If we are souls who know that we live in order to die and be with God, why the fear?

MARY: My dear one, as humans, you also have a shadow side, a side of you that can bring in darkness, thus allowing fear. This darkness is not from God but from the energies that are in opposition to all that is good. Yes, the soul knows, but the mind fights this wisdom. And so, people forget heaven, and a fear of the unknown comes in. Yet, with faith, heaven and the truth of death become known. When people truly know God, they know that heaven does exist and there is no fear. It all stems from knowing God.

ANNA: I don't want to digress, so I will ask you more about the shadow side later. You mention that the soul knows . . . Does the soul know all past lives and all that it has gone through?

MARY: Yes, the soul remembers, yet as a human being you are not privy to all these memories. Your soul will guide you through the lessons it has learned in the past, but the memories themselves are not always conscious.

ANNA: But they can come through, can't they? Isn't that déjà vu?

MARY: Yes, memories can surface through déjà vu and dreams and when meeting someone that you may have known in a past life.

ANNA: Does this explain the notion of meeting someone and feeling like you have known them forever?

MARY: Yes, souls reincarnate with other souls; they have a pact to teach and guide each other.

ANNA: What if the relationship of these souls fails or brings pain?

MARY: My daughter, humans must go through pain to evolve. Pain always brings lessons. Be grateful for the good and the challenging lessons in your lives. It is the reaction to the pain that may bring you closer to God and the perfection of your soul. It is difficult not to become bitter in a world so full of tragedy and suffering. Surrender the joy and pain to God, and allow the love to come in and heal you.

ANNA: None of us like the pain . . . Some people suffer so much more than others. Why is that?

MARY: Every soul is different and must go its own path in order to reach heaven. So much is grounded in free will and past lifetimes. Before the soul reincarnates, while in the heavenly realm, it agrees to what it must experience on earth.

ANNA: Thank you for sharing this with me. You speak of heaven where there is no fear, anger, or hate. Yet, there is so much of that in this world. Can you talk to me of this?

MARY: Yes. It is necessary to speak of things in order for the world to heal.

Meditation for Chapter Six

✦ Gently close your eyes and breathe. Ask the angels to surround you in a brilliant circle of light, love, and protection. Imagine a column of light from heaven moving into the crown of your head, spreading through your body, and anchoring you to the core of the earth. Feel this wonderful light moving through your spinal column up from the tips of your toes. Allow your body to relax as you focus on your breath. Be aware of the rise and fall of your chest as you breathe in all that is good and right in the universe. Be aware that you are filling your lungs with the Divine breath of God. Imagine your breath as a gentle wave moving back and forth and back and forth. Feel your body relax after each exhale as you release stress, negativity, and all else that doesn't serve you. Be conscious of how wonderful this feels. It is truly a gift to permit relaxation and peace into your body, soul, and mind.

✦ Allow the energy of Mary, of her love and peace, to enter your body with each inhale. Exhale all that doesn't serve you; all stress, anxiety, anger, animosity, self-recrimination, and anything else that might get in the way of connecting to heaven. As you move into that wonderful place of total relaxation begin to feel a sensation of peace moving through your body. It feels wonderful. Bask in this relaxation and peace. As you continue to feel the rise and fall of your chest as you breathe, imagine there is a silky pale blue light encircling your body. You feel its gentle vibration as it swirls around you, alerting and filling your senses. Just allow yourself to be, as this blue vibration floats around you. Know that it is good. Let this vibration hug you gently. Recognize this vibration to be Mother Mary. Let her warm presence move your focus from your breath to the soft beating of your heart.

✦ Envision your heart becoming larger in your chest as you let her in. See the soft blue that is circling around you, and allow it to enter your physical body and your heart. Imagine that your whole being is reaching out to her. As you allow the soft blue light to fill your heart, recognize that both you and Mary are blending energetically; you are becoming one essence. Delight in knowing that you are vibrating with her energy. As you breathe, begin to feel her more and more and allow yourself to go deeper. Now imagine a clear space, free of thought, and allow your breath to wander in silence. Visualize Mary standing in front of you; whatever image that works best is fine. She can continue to be the pale blue light or a feeling, or perhaps you may want to personify her. Again, whatever seems right or feels

right. See her reaching out her hand or see her energy
expanding toward you.

+ Hear her speak softly: "There is no death." Feel her
  warm touch as she tenderly leads you through a wide,
  ancient doorway, engraved with words written in
  Hebrew and Arabic, into an empty yet brilliantly lit
  room. She tells you that this room holds the energy of
  heaven. You hear the angels singing and others chanting
  as the music soothes and lulls you. You feel relaxed
  and happy as the immense joy of love surrounds you.
  Mary asks you to open your heart, to let go of fear and
  welcome the love that brings heaven into your mind,
  body, and soul. Sit in this place of love, peace, and joy
  for as long as you desire. Take this feeling with you as
  you go about your day. When you forget, come back to
  this place and this meditation.

7

Evil in the World

What Is Evil?

ANNA: Mother, if God created all in love, where does evil come from?

MARY: My dearest, evil so hurts me. When humans act in a way to hurt themselves and others it is in direct opposition to the will of God and all that is love. Evil has existed for almost as long as humankind, yet there wasn't evil in the beginning; evil grew out of a human desire to have dominance over one another and to want things that were not of God. People moved from the purity of love into a place where the things that they created and the power that could be achieved in life became very important. This evil created competition to gain more money and more power. A fight for supremacy emerged in many areas of their lives. Evil is not in power or money, but in how it is used to corrupt the goodness of God.

ANNA: It seems to me that power gives people the illusion of control over their lives. Is that evil?

MARY: If only people would have faith, they would not suffer anxiety for the lack of control in their lives. People seek to be in control since so much is out of their control. They believe that there will be peace if they can control all around them. That will never be. But, if they would surrender to the will of God in prayer and accept the power that is above all, there would be no need to make gods of themselves. It is not only idolatry of things and money, but of themselves. Many people strive to become a god but not like God. In the quest for supremacy, they feed their egos with things and money and power to impress people. They seek praise and their pride grows. They worship themselves and not the Divine within. It is not evil to desire control, but it is the means to find control that lead to evil ways. And the evil force in the universe will tempt people to stray from righteousness and to that which does not serve Love.

ANNA: I am not sure I understand. If God didn't create this evil force and it goes against all that he is, why does he allow it?

MARY: My daughter, be patient with me . . . this is so difficult for you to conceptualize. You and all people were created in the beauty of love and all that is good. God created people in all his glory to share in his love. Yet, this creation also allowed evil in as a way for people to be able to choose the right path to the heart of God. Without the dark we would not know the light. How could you know the wonders of the light of day without the darkness of night? It is that simple.

ANNA: Well, I wish there was a better way. There is so much about evil that I don't understand. You say that we were created in beauty and love. Through my studies in psychology, I have learned about the "shadow side" which Swiss psychiatrist Carl Jung said is part of who we are. To simplify, he said that we have an aspect of our personality that is dark because it is made of negative, socially, or religiously inferior human emotions and impulses like sexual lust, power strivings, selfishness, greed, envy, anger, or rage. It seems that whatever we see as bad or unacceptable and that which we deny in ourselves, becomes part of the shadow. Is it true that we have a dark side?

MARY: My dear, this is very complicated but I will help you to understand. All people are born pure and good. As time goes on, because the world is filled with both good and bad, children learn to distinguish between the two. People desire not just the good, but the bad as well. These desires become a part of the person and what you are referring to as the shadow side. This side of the person forms cravings for that which is not of God. This is also the foundation of free will and choice. Each person must choose to follow the part of their nature that is in accord with that of God's, or the other side which feeds their want of that in the world outside of God's goodness.

ANNA: So another way of looking at what you are talking about is morality . . .

MARY: Morality is the right way of living. People should follow Love and it will all be right. The way to live morally is written in the Ten Commandments and is spoken of in the precepts of the religions. To love and respect yourself and others . . . to love God above all. If all people lived following this simple rule, the people of the world would unite and there would be peace.

ANNA: So that makes me wonder if there is evil inside us. Are we not such good people?

MARY: My dear! You are beings of the light, God is moral and most perfect in his goodness. Yet, you have within you the ability to choose to do things against your nature. It is a constant battle of humankind . . . to act out of what is right and pleases the Lord, or do the opposite. It is the battle to follow God and join in his love and all that is perfect and right in the universe. Again, it goes back to free will. God, in his wisdom, knows how difficult this can be and revels when people choose to follow him and what is good. And it is true that not everyone chooses the right path. There are those who choose to give in to the dark. In doing so, they attract the evil forces outside of themselves.

ANNA: Many religions believe there is a primary force in the world that is evil. In Zoroastrianism it is called Ahriman, in Buddhism it is Mara, in Judaism and Christianity it is called Satan, Lucifer, or the Devil. In Islam it is Shaitan or Iblis; even Norse religions identify this evil as Nidhogg. Is this true? Is there really a "devil"?

MARY: The world evolved in balance and God did not stop this. And so, in that balance is the good and the bad. Arising from man's desire for material things of the world and also to be supreme, a force emerged that is pure evil and can be called by any of these names.

ANNA: These religions put forth so many views of what this evil energy is. What is the Truth?

MARY: My daughter, I am so pleased that you so long for the Truth. Yet, sometimes the Truth is mingled together with different viewpoints or sources. In this instance, each religion puts forth a truth about the Evil One. Each name and depiction of evil is correct. Within each tradition there are minor differences but all speak of the evil energy or force that exists and pulls people from God. This force can enter into the hearts and minds of people and allow destruction.

ANNA: How does this "evil" pull people from God?

MARY: My son prayed, "And lead us not into temptation, but deliver us from evil" (Matthew 6:13). This evil he spoke of lures people from what is good, right, and moral to that which feeds the other side of themselves, the darker side you speak of. It can lure and influence people with worldly riches and short-term happiness toward immediate gratification. God promises eternal happiness filled with the riches of his kingdom. Evil cannot do that. It doesn't bring love, it brings self-destruction and defilement. It brings hatred and anger which are products of fear. Through the ages it has lured people from the one true path to Love. The Evil One promised my son dominion over all if only he would worship him. My son said to him, "Away with you, Satan! For it is written, 'You shall worship the Lord your God, and Him only you shall serve'" (Matthew 4:10–11).

ANNA: Jesus knew it was the Devil tempting him, but what about people who can use rationalization, and don't see evil for what it is? Osama bin Laden, through his extremist viewpoint, caused so much pain and was responsible for so many deaths. Many people believed him when he talked about how right it was to hate and purge Americans, Jews, and Christians. Now we have other groups who have risen up to do the same. How can they not understand and have compassion for the people they are hurting in the name of God?

MARY: My daughter, evil can truly never be rationalized. God gave people the ability to do so but he also gave people intelligence and grace to know the difference between good and bad. How can it ever be rationalized that it is good to destroy a race of people? How can killing and mutilating ever be good? Evil is evil and so it is. Also, as I have mentioned, fear is the opposite of love. Osama bin Laden, through the evil that moved within him, knew this. The Evil One works with and through fear. Bin Laden instilled fear in his people—fear that the "others" would take over the world and leave his people behind; fear that his people were losing their power. It was fear, not love, that motivated the atrocities and that is what evil does and always has done.

ANNA: Okay, I presented an extreme example. In everyday life people are pulled away from their families to make more money and buy more things. They are tempted by the things of the world to bring them happiness. They may not see this as an evil force, pulling them away from the Truth of God. They may rationalize this as needing money to survive and that money brings happiness. How do we handle these challenges?

MARY: That is an excellent question as it applies to so many people. Anything that pulls one away from God is evil. Greed is evil. People must strive to live in peace with the riches of God. This greed or want for more and more and more becomes like an infection spreading through the person, which will kill their essence and, more importantly, their relationship with God. The infection spreads to the manner in which they conduct themselves and they may become arrogant and only speak of money and the things that they own. They may follow evil and become obsessed. Yet, in the end, they own nothing and may have lost everything.

ANNA: Will God forgive these people for their actions?

MARY: God forgives all who come to him on bended knee in search for forgiveness.

ANNA: If that is true, and supposing that evil is an entity, can that entity receive forgiveness?

MARY: Oh, my daughter, how wonderful that would be! If the Devil someday seeks redemption, so be it. God is all loving and will grant forgiveness even to the Devil himself! The cessation of evil would be the saving of the human race!

ANNA: Some people have said that there is a duality in God; a good side and a not so good side. Is there a dark side to God?

MARY: I have said to you and you must know in your heart and your mind that God is a being of pure Love. I know, my child, how difficult it is to know that there can be a being that is only good and only made of Love. You cannot see this with your eyes but must know it in your heart for it is Truth. God is only Love. He does not cause pain. God does not have any darkness or evil attached to him. The duality is in what the world created. God is the "I Am" and nothing more. He is who is and in that is the composition of complete love and benevolence. Think nothing more of God and you will understand all about his nature. You also must pray to God to protect you.

ANNA: I am praying. Mother Mary, please pray with me.

MARY: I shall pray and I am with you.

ANNA: What about material things? I admit that I like nice things and the world is filled with objects. In order to buy things people need to work and make money. Is it wrong to want material things and money?

MARY: You live in a world where money is used to purchase things. God wants his children to live in abundance. He didn't create this, it happened over time and it is understandable how it came about. It is what is done with the money that is troubling. Money and things are not to be worshipped. Only God and love are to be held in the highest. In the end, the things that money buys will vanish. It is the love that remains for eternity.

ANNA: So, Mother, does that mean that we can all get to heaven even if we have a wealth of possessions?

MARY: Yes, my daughter, heaven is open to those who love themselves and each other and recognize and adore the Creator. But please, I must repeat that only God is to be worshipped. Only God can fill the void and yearning for love and completeness, not the things of the world. And until you are in paradise, there will always be people with more and those with less material wealth. Yet, it is right and compassionate to provide and help those who are in more need. If a man needs a coat, tear your coat in two and both you and this man will be kept warm.

ANNA: So there should be no guilt about wanting material things?

MARY: *Guilt* is a word used to control people. People impose it on others and then on themselves. There should be no guilt about wanting and attaining things. Obtaining things of the world cannot become a reason for existence. The reason for existence is to love; to accept love and share love, in order to become closer to God. If money and things of the world get in the way of this journey, then it is not a good thing and will result in a separation from God.

ANNA: So is guilt is a bad thing?

MARY: Guilt is not bad in and of itself. It happens when people feel that they have done something that is against the will of God; against the morality that they follow. It goes hand in hand with shame. God is a forgiving force. Because people live within the realm of free will, there is always cause and effect. Yet, when people are truly contrite, God forgives all who come to him with a contrite heart and a sincere desire to be cleansed of their sins or wrongdoings.

ANNA: What about sin? It is a word that sometimes is used more than *love* within religions. I understand the message is always to turn away from sin, but I wish that love would be spoken of more often within the houses of God.

MARY: The focus of humankind should always be on love. That will stop the transgressions or sins of people. That will stop the evil that abounds in the world. And yes, the temples and churches should preach love above all else since that is the way to the heart of God. Focusing on the sins and not how to bring love into communities, families, and the world is not productive. If the focus is love, there will be a diminishing of wrongdoing and more unity with God. People should be taught how to live in concert with each other with love. Leave the evil for the Evil One. The sins should not be given energy. All energy should be on love. Those who preach about God should be preaching love. Not love that has boundaries, for that is not love. Rather love that is universal. It is so simple and what you all need to know.

ANNA: It says in the Old Testament that children will be punished for the sins of their fathers. This seems very unfair. Is it true?

MARY: Each person is given a chance to go to the light or the dark. God does not punish. People punish themselves. When one dies, it is in reviewing their lives that punishment and pain may occur. God does not impose that. Yet, if a child chooses to follow the steps of his father who is sinful, both will suffer. Also, in reading any holy text, be aware of situations that the words speak to; these words are sometimes specific to the situation or story being told. People must be careful of misuse and misinterpretation or taking words out of context. In the biblical text that you are referring to, God is speaking of the sin of idolatry. Idolatry is a betrayal of God. And, the Evil One, at that time, was trying to integrate idolatry into that culture as a replacement for God.

Over time, the children who were raised with this form of worship would continue the practice and teach their own children the practice. And so it would go on and perpetuate this transgression against God. And so parents, please teach your children what is good and right, which will arm them with energetic weapons to combat the evil in the world. Then your teachings will perpetuate and your children will be saved . . .

ANNA: Along this line, prayer was taken out of public schools in the United States. Is it okay if children are taught to just pray at home or in their churches or temples?

MARY: Prayer belongs everywhere! God belongs everywhere! It doesn't need to be a prayer of any one religion, it can be a silent prayer of the heart. There is no place that prayer and adoring God should be prohibited.

ANNA: You have said to the children at Fatima, ". . . the Rosary is my Power . . . It is the weapon which you must make use of in these times of the Great Battle . . . Every Rosary which you recite with me has the effect of restricting the action of the Evil One, of drawing souls away from his pernicious influence . . . and of expanding goodness in my children." And you said to Simon Stock, "Pray and let the Rosary always be in your hands as a sign to Satan that you belong to me." Should all people say the Rosary, even those who are not Catholic?

MARY: The Rosary is a powerful weapon against evil. It is not only in the prayers said on the beads, but in the energy it creates in the repetition of the prayers. The prayers become a mantra and raise the vibration in and around all who say it. It also brings me closer as I will say it with you. All can say the Rosary, yet the words in the prayers may not be consistent with their religious beliefs. And so, I say, change the wording if that will make it right for you.

ANNA: There are specific Catholic prayers recited in the Rosary. How can those be changed?

MARY: Each person should make these prayers consistent with what they believe. The Nicene Creed is a statement of faith; say your own statement. The Glory Be to the Father prayer is a prayer to glorify God and his presence through the ages that can be made consistent with other belief systems.

ANNA: Can animals embody evil? People often say pit bulls are evil animals.

MARY: Animals cannot be evil since they don't have the intelligence and are not equipped to make choices. Yet, it is deplorable that people raise animals to be vicious and mean. Animals are innocent beings and cannot be evil. Most domesticated animals only want to be loved and to love their masters. Animals in the wild follow their natural instincts to survive and protect themselves and their young with aggression. That is not evil but justifiable given the laws of nature. I pray that animals are not used as weapons or harmed in any way in order to make money. It is the one who is using animals in this way who is going against God. God loves all his creations and all must be treated with love and kindness.

ANNA: Blessed Mother, what are we to do to eliminate all the evil in the world? How can we protect ourselves and our children?

MARY: Pray, chant, and adore God above all else. Pray for courage in your children so that they will be able to walk away from temptation. Most religions have prayers of protection from the Evil One. The Hindus chant the Mahamrityunjaya Mantra, which is said to ward off evil. Divine vibrations are generated by intoning this chant to ward off all the negative and evil forces. These vibrations create a powerful protective shield. Muslims say a prayer in the morning to ward off evil and believe that the prayer protects from evil from morning until the end of the day, when it is said again to protect from evil as one sleeps. I say to you, pray, pray, and pray in whatever way makes sense for you! Ask for the archangel Michael to shield and protect you and your loved ones. I will pray with you.

Meditation for Chapter Seven

✦ Gently close your eyes and breathe. Ask the angels to surround you in a brilliant circle of light, love, and protection. Imagine a column of light from heaven moving into the crown of your head, spreading through your body, and anchoring you to the core of the earth. Feel this wonderful light moving through your spinal column up from the tips of your toes. Allow your body to relax as you focus on your breath. Be aware of the rise and fall of your chest as you breathe in all that is good and right in the universe. Be aware that you are filling your lungs with the Divine breath of God. Imagine your breath as a gentle wave moving back and forth and back and forth. Feel your body relax after each exhale as you release stress, negativity, and all else that doesn't serve you. Be conscious of how wonderful this feels. It is truly a gift to permit relaxation and peace into your body, soul, and mind.

✦ Allow the energy of Mary, of her love and peace, to enter your body with each inhale. Exhale all that doesn't serve you; all stress, anxiety, anger, animosity, self-recrimination, and anything else that might get in the way of connecting to heaven. As you move into that wonderful place of total relaxation begin to feel a sensation of peace moving through your body. It feels wonderful. Bask in this relaxation and peace. As you continue to feel the rise and fall of your chest as you breathe, imagine there is a silky pale blue light encircling your body. You feel its gentle vibration as it swirls around you, alerting and filling your senses. Just allow yourself to be, as this blue vibration floats around you. Know that it is good. Let this vibration hug you gently. Recognize this vibration to be Mother Mary. Let her warm presence move your focus from your breath to the soft beating of your heart.

+ Envision your heart becoming larger in your chest as you let her in. See the soft blue that is circling around you ease into your physical body and your heart. Imagine that your whole being is reaching out to her to be a part of her. As you allow the soft blue light to fill your heart, recognize that both you and Mary are blending energetically; you are becoming one essence. Delight in knowing that you are vibrating with her energy. As you breathe, begin to feel her more and more and allow yourself to go deeper. Now imagine a clear space, free of thought, and allow your breath to wander in silence. Visualize Mary standing in front of you; whatever image that works best for you is fine. She can continue to be the pale blue light or a feeling, or perhaps you may want to personify her. Again whatever seems right or feels right. See her reaching out her hand or see her energy expanding toward you.

✦ Hear her say, "Release all fear, self-loathing, hate, addictive behavior, unkind thoughts, and anything else that does not serve you from your mind, body, and spirit." Feel all these negative attributes begin to leave you. Allow your mind and body to fill this vacant space with compassion, love, peace, faith, hope, and forgiveness. As you do so, begin to feel lighter as you are no longer chained to all that is not good in the world. Hear Mary tell you there is only one God and he is a power of love and compassion. Hear her ask you to allow him into your heart. As you listen to her words, begin to feel an unconditional love fill you from head to toe. Then say, "I release all feelings and all actions that I have been involved in that do not serve Love." Bask in the feeling of pure love.

8

Angels

Do They Really Exist? What Are They?

ANNA: Mother, please tell me about the angels.

MARY: Angels are glorious creatures. They fill the kingdom of God, and by doing so, give glory to God. They were created in the beginning and exist now and forever. They have always been a part of the realm of God. They mingle with the vibration of God as pure beings of light.

ANNA: And so is the purpose of angels simply to give glory to God?

MARY: The role of angels has changed over the eons. As the world changed, and man evolved, their purpose has also evolved and expanded. Today, they serve not only God but all people.

ANNA: What are they like?

MARY: They are wonderful beings of light and goodness. Angels have never been human; they have always been pure light. They are bright like the sun and as light as a feather. They float in and around people and God. They are the attendants of Truth. They are such benevolent beings that help, guide, and protect, and bring God's love to all people. Angels are God's messengers and teachers. They carry great wisdom bestowed upon them from God. Their tasks are of high importance and carry a high vibration to people. The angels come to announce, lead, and speak of God's love. The angel Gabriel appeared to Daniel in the Old Testament, Zechariah in the New Testament, and Muhammed in the Quran. The angels come forward in all religions to light the way to the one Truth.

ANNA: You say they are in God's kingdom. How then do they serve us here on earth?

MARY: Like all spirits, they can be both in the kingdom and on earth.

ANNA: How do they help us here?

MARY: My dear, people are in desperate need of help from heaven! The angels sometimes act as a conscience, influencing what is right. They may speak to people in dreams or even use the voice of other people to convey messages. Sometimes they appear visually to people who are open spiritually to them. They are always around.

ANNA: Is it true that each one of us has a guardian angel of our own? Can we have more than one guardian angel?

MARY: Every person has their own guardian angel who guides and teaches them specifically. They are mostly earth bound so that they can constantly help their charges. There is help from heaven arriving every moment! Open your eyes to see; open your ears to hear! You are all surrounded by many other angels who also protect you. You are never alone.

ANNA: Are our guardian angels with us all the time?

MARY: Yes, they never leave you. They surround you in their love and light.

ANNA: How do our guardian angels get assigned to us?

MARY: Your guardian angel has had a relationship with you since the time your soul was born. Your guardian angel knows your soul and every aspect of your being, including your past lives, your thoughts, motivations, desires, and needs. You are so loved by this being! Your guardian angel exists for your soul's growth.

ANNA: What happens to our guardian angels when we die?

MARY: They continue to stay with you and teach you. Their experience with God is different than yours. In the afterlife they share this knowledge and love with you.

ANNA: What happens when we veer from what is good?

MARY: They recognize your ego and pray for you. They try to influence you through your conscious and unconscious mind. They bring others to you to help.

ANNA: What about other angels? Are they around me as well?

MARY: Angels circle around you and all people. They are around you to support you and lift you up. They help to change your vibration and connection to the Divine. Each person has an army of protection around them.

ANNA: And yet we continue to get ourselves in trouble!

MARY: Ahh . . . free will. You may hear the right things and still do the wrong things.

ANNA: Can angels direct our lives?

MARY: They can only help to keep you on your path, and close to God. They teach and guide. Their task is to show each person the way to reach God and to live in the abundance of God's grace and love.

ANNA: Do angels have souls?

MARY: Again, my dear, angels are different than humans. Like humans, they are the extension of God's love, yet they are pure and wanting for nothing else but to be in God's graces and to give him praise and adoration.

ANNA: Is it true that there are fallen angels?

MARY: In the beginning, there were those who believed they could have their own kingdom apart from God. So the answer is yes. They manifested ego. They became the opposing force.

ANNA: Can that happen again?

MARY: Of course, angels, too, have free will. Yet, it is unlikely since the angels have been around since the beginning and relish in the light and love of God.

ANNA: Do pets have guardian angels?

MARY: There are angels who surround animals, yet since animals don't have the intelligence of a human being, they are not responsive to being guided by angels. The angels who surround them act as a blanket of love. Animals are very intuitive and feel them.

ANNA: Are there specific angels assigned to specific jobs? For instance, is there an angel for travel or angel for doctors and nurses?

MARY: Somewhat. Angels are drawn to certain activities or professions, just like humans, but it is not so precise since all angels can help in all situations.

ANNA: So it isn't necessary to call in the "angel of writers" as I write this book?

MARY: My dear, you aren't writing this book!

ANNA: Okay, if I were writing a book without you?

MARY: You don't specifically need to call in the "angel of writers." Yet, you may call in the angels and ask them to surround you as you work. They will influence your writing for your highest good and the good of all that are touched by it. This is true of all things. You may call them in when you are experiencing a conflict with your employer and ask for guidance and clarity.

ANNA: What is the best way to talk to angels?

MARY: It is helpful if you remember they have never been human. They take words very literarily. Questions need to be posed in the most specific way possible.

ANNA: Okay. So how, exactly, do angels communicate with people?

MARY: They communicate many ways. They may be a voice in a person's mind. They may move objects. You may see them as a beautiful, magnificent, bright white light. They feel very light and tend to suspend themselves above. They want to be wanted. Talk to them and call them into your life for protection and guidance. They love you.

ANNA: Many people talk about seeing angels. How do they appear to people?

MARY: Angels appear to people all the time! They want people to know that they are not alone. They are beings of soft light. Their density is like a feather. They hover in the corners. Some people may see a twinkling light floating . . . or if you look out into a room, you may see breaks in the light around you. Angels are the light. There are millions of them around you and everyone. They fill the atmosphere and cushion you.

ANNA: What about really seeing them? Do they have wings?

MARY: Angels are weightless and seem to fly. Yet, these wonderful creatures do not actually have wings. Occasionally they appear with wings so that they are recognized by humans. But, truly, they just float. There is no reason for wings—it is a human concept to explain how they can fly or float. Most often angels appear as a brilliant light that gives off love and peace.

ANNA: Also, some have said they have seen angels manifested as another individual. How can that be if they have never been human?

MARY: Angels will do what they can to help. Sometimes that means taking a human form temporarily.

ANNA: Perhaps to save someone from an accident?

MARY: If it isn't the person's time to pass on to the kingdom, of course. Angels are strong in all ways and can lift a person from a crumbled car or restart a heartbeat. Always be in gratitude for those in heaven who help you. They are filled with joy knowing that their help is recognized. When you thank them, you are giving gratitude to God who sent them to you.

ANNA: Do they have names?

MARY: Yes, they are named.

ANNA: How can we find out our guardian's name?

MARY: Meditate, quiet your mind, and ask.

ANNA: How do we know if it is the right name?

MARY: You make me smile. How do you know if it is the wrong name? Feel it and you will know. Believe.

ANNA: Do they mind if we call them the wrong name?

MARY: They only want you to call them.

ANNA: Some people have spoken of angels taking them on journeys through the astral plane as they sleep. Do they do that?

MARY: Yes, as one sleeps the soul is set free to learn and heal. This is a glorious experience although not always necessary for the person to remember when he or she is awake. These journeys are for the benefit of the soul's development. The angels, spirit guides, and other heavenly entities accompany the soul on these journeys.

ANNA: It is so good to know we are never alone.

MARY: You are so loved and you will never be alone. Talk to the angels and listen to their song. They are everywhere you go.

Meditation for Chapter Eight

+ Gently close your eyes and breathe. Ask the angels to surround you in a brilliant circle of light, love, and protection. Imagine a column of light from heaven moving into the crown of your head, spreading through your body, and anchoring you to the core of the earth. Feel this wonderful light moving through your spinal column up from the tips of your toes. Allow your body to relax as you focus on your breath. Be aware of the rise and fall of your chest as you breathe in all that is good and right in the universe. Be aware that you are filling your lungs with the Divine breath of God. Imagine your breath as a gentle wave moving back and forth and back and forth. Feel your body relax after each exhale as you release stress, negativity, and all else that doesn't serve you. Be conscious of how wonderful this feels. It is truly a gift to permit relaxation and peace into your mind, body, and soul.

✦ Allow the energy of Mary, of her love and peace, to enter your body with each inhale. Exhale all that doesn't serve you; all stress, anxiety, anger, animosity, self-recrimination, and anything else that might get in the way of connecting to heaven. As you move into that wonderful place of total relaxation, begin to feel a sensation of peace moving through your body. It feels wonderful. Bask in this peace and relax. As you continue to feel the rise and fall of your chest as you breathe, imagine there is a silky pale blue light encircling your body. You feel its gentle vibration as it swirls around you, alerting and filling your senses. Just allow yourself to be, as this blue vibration floats around you. Know that it is good. Let this vibration hug you gently. Recognize this vibration to be Mother Mary. Let her warm presence move your focus from your breath to the soft beating of your heart. Envision your heart becoming larger in your chest as you let her in. See the soft blue that is circling around you, and ease it into your physical body and your heart. Imagine that your whole being is reaching out to her. As you allow the soft blue light to fill your heart, recognize that both you and Mary are blending energetically; you are becoming one essence. Delight in knowing that you are vibrating with her energy. As you breathe, begin to feel her more and more and allow yourself to go deeper. Now imagine a clear space, free of thought, and allow your breath to wander in silence. Visualize Mary standing in front of you; whatever image that works best for you is fine. She can continue to be the pale blue light or a feeling, or perhaps you may want to personify her. Again whatever seems right or feels right.

+ See her or feel her as she beckons you. Follow her into a beautiful meadow. Feel the verdant lush green grass beneath your feet and look up to a clear, azure blue sky. The golden rays of the sun caress your head and shoulders as you walk with her through this meadow. After a bit, she indicates that you should sit on the ground and breathe in the wonders of nature that you are so much a part of. She stands behind you. As you take in all that is around you, you see flickering lights just ahead of you. One light is brighter and bigger than the rest. As it gets closer, you feel an undeniable connection. The light may begin to take on a form. As it is now upon you, you know this to be your guardian angel.

+ This wonderful being sits next to you and begins to communicate with you telepathically. You ask this angel questions such as its name or why it is your angel. You talk about different things going on in your life. You empty your heart as well as your mind. When you feel as though the conversation is over, you stand and your angel stands with you. Mary, your angel, and you walk together in the meadow.

+ When you are ready, you open your eyes with the knowledge that you are never truly walking alone.

9

Enlightenment

What Is an Awakening?

ANNA: Although the term *enlightenment* is not prevalent in Christianity or Judaism, it has become ubiquitous in our society, particularly with the birth of various New Age therapies and modern spirituality. Buddhists are known for using the term *enlightenment*, which, I have learned, is actually the Western translation of *Bodhi*, which means "an awakening." Therefore, depending on which religion or spirituality that one subscribes to, enlightenment seems to mean a variety of things: an awakening, the practice of finding oneself and/or shedding one's past, reaching a spiritual place similar to nirvana, and so on and so forth. My naive understanding, in how it applies to our relationship with God, or how I'd like to think it applies to that relationship, is that enlightenment is a conscious recognition of being one essence with God, thus enabling us to transcend the desires of the material world. The long and the short of it is—is there such a state of being?

MARY: Yes, there is such a state of being! The mystics through the ages have aspired for this state of being! They have wanted to purge themselves of the worldly desires to be in union with God. They have sought to find the power of God within their beings. Spiritual enlightenment conveys a level of wisdom and knowledge about life and the universe that cannot be achieved in any other way other than by dying and being reborn in heaven. The enlightenment brings complete understanding of life and the universe as one detaches from material things.

ANNA: That sounds like a monumental task! Can one actually reach this state while living in this world?

MARY: It may seem unfathomable but, yes, one can reach this state. It is usually an evolved soul that has gone through many lifetimes who will attain this state. Reaching this state means moving from the desires of the physical body into that of the soul's desires which are solely focused on God. Yes, it is difficult for people to achieve this state, or even understand it, given the various distractions of the world. Your media speaks of wars, people striving for power, crimes against humanity, and the like. Yet, it does not address all that is good on a daily basis. Yes, there are people all around the world consciously seeking enlightenment. They are from various religions and walks of life. Not all achieve this state, but there are great blessings bestowed upon those who attempt to reach it.

ANNA: Was Jesus enlightened?

MARY: Jesus was indeed enlightened! Jesus knew the Father resided within his physical being. Sometimes people forget that Jesus was of flesh and blood and had to fight the temptations of the world. Yet, he stood firm in his truth which is the Truth of God. He rejected all that wasn't from the Father. He lived to fulfill the will of God; and so he did. His teachings and his words live on and will continue to do so. He sought not the power of being adored on earth. He sought to teach people the way to enlightenment; the way to God. If all people would follow the words of my son, there would be peace. Earth would cease to exist and all people would live in the kingdom. I pray for this day.

ANNA: Was Jesus able to perform miracles because of his enlightenment?

MARY: He was able to perform miracles because he recognized the power of God flowing through him. He told his disciples that they could do the same. I tell you this: If you believe that the power of God is in you and you have no fear but act in love and compassion, you, too, will be able to will bring forward miracles. With pure faith in God you can make the mountains sing!

ANNA: Was the Buddha enlightened?

MARY: Like Jesus, Siddhartha (Buddha) could not be frightened and was tempted not only by the material things of the world but by evil. In his meditation he connected with the essence of the universe. Through this process of going into his soul and all that is in the universe, he became enlightened. There are many similarities to my son: He did not seek glorification; it is in his teachings that the world can be saved; he spoke of compassion and love and of the noble truths to build good character. In his state of enlightenment, the Truth was known and he sought to bring others to that place.

ANNA: Were you enlightened?

MARY: Yes, I was enlightened and deeply connected to God. I didn't want for material goods. I spend much time with God in prayer. I heard the voice of God and the angels. My faith was a testament to the life I lived. I spoke the words of God and those of my son and spread the teachings without fear. Yet, I was not at the level of Jesus or Buddha.

ANNA: Are there several levels of enlightenment?

MARY: The highest level of enlightenment is to forgo all fear and all desires and live in the light and share the wisdom of being in the light with the world. The material world has no place for those who are at the highest level of enlightenment. It is a true knowledge of God and Divinity within.

ANNA: I know we spoke about souls, but can you digress and speak to me about the levels of soul growth?

MARY: There is no digression as all topics are one topic! For each soul this varies, but in general I will pass on the wisdom. I will give the levels names so that you will understand and remember. Know that sometimes it may take many years to go from one level to the next and there may be levels in between. It is not precise as each soul is unique and goes through their evolution differently. I will be clear and concise for you to learn, yet I will be brief. There is so much more to say about this that you will be able to write another book. Also, one level is not so neatly defined from another; they sometimes blend one into another.

- In the first level, the soul is an infant. Similar to a baby, it must learn about physical existence, life, and death, and has a need to be nurtured. Sometimes it can be egocentric.
- In the second level, the soul is more like a child, it knows about the world it lives in—its society and culture—but it seeks a place within it all. It wants to belong.
- In the third level, the soul is similar to an adolescent and must learn about free will, responsibility for itself, and fortitude.
- In the fourth level, the soul is mature and must learn how to live with other people.

As a "Mature Soul," it has learned about coexistence and compassion and love as it exists on the earth. It must now learn tolerance and patience.

+ The fifth level represents the level of "old soul." The old soul has learned, and gone through, all of the levels above. It is ready to become one with God.

ANNA: Are there many old souls walking the earth at this level today?

MARY: Blessed be God, yes! That is why the world is more open to the voice of heaven.

ANNA: So if I was an old soul what would I have to do to reach this unity with God?

MARY: You must surrender to God; recognize his great love and truly love and have compassion for yourself and others. You must give up the cravings of the ego and sit in prayer and meditation to connect with God. You must live your life in accordance with the will of God.

ANNA: When one reaches this level, are they finished cycling through lifetimes?

MARY: Yes, they may stay in the realm. Yet, if they choose to reenter the earth to teach and help, they may do that as well.

ANNA: So in order to become enlightened, do we have to quit our jobs and mediate all day like the Tibetan monks?

MARY: The Tibetan monks seek enlightenment in one way, while you may in another. You may keep your job, yet if the job or your role in it does not, in some way, raise the vibration of the world, then it would be challenging for you to achieve enlightenment. An old soul who seeks enlightenment will engage in activities that provide personal fulfillment. This could be in areas such as art, gardening, writing, or things that ignite a passion. Then, toward the end of the level, the old soul seeks to help and teach others about the way to God. It may then be ready for enlightenment.

ANNA: In order to reach enlightenment, do we have to give up all our worldly possessions?

MARY: Ahhh . . . the part that is most difficult to think about! You would not need to give them all up but they would need to have less meaning to you. You would need to define yourself by the Love you carry in your heart, not your possessions. You would shift from a focus on material things to a focus on God and his essence. You may be surprised at just how much of your life is composed of material things and yet startled at how, with a devotion to God, these things would lose their luster for you.

ANNA: When I picture an enlightened being, I imagine a guru. Seriously, could I actually reach that status?

MARY: What is a guru but a teacher? Words! As an enlightened being you would teach others about love, compassion, God, and Truth in the same way other enlightened masters have. You could do this in your work and with the people you know. As I said, there isn't one right way. Buddha was brought up in Brahmanism and Jesus was a Jew. They spoke in a way that their own people could hear and understand. All who seek enlightenment must learn how to spread God's message in a way that is right and good for them and the people around them.

ANNA: Do I have to become enlightened to get to heaven?

MARY: In order to live in God's realm, you must be compassionate to yourself and others. You must follow the Truth and Love, which embodies all that is God. And if you don't, you will go through your life review and return to the earth to attempt to learn once again.

ANNA: That's good! I will try my best to be compassionate, but now I feel less pressure to become enlightened.

MARY: That "pressure" of which you speak is the ego's fear of failure. Fear not and love more.

ANNA: You speak of spreading love through enlightenment and loving oneself. What does that really mean?

MARY: Part of loving yourself means giving up a piece of the "self." In loving yourself, you seek to know who you are and your individual truth. Your truth is who you are as a being of God. Your soul knows this truth well and attempts to bring this out of you. Your ego, the self, is fearful of the suffering your truth may cause you. The self is in denial of the power of God. When you find your truth and embrace it, the ego will step back and you can fully love yourself. When you can feel and see the beauty of God within, you can love not only yourself but others. This is the ultimate power on earth . . . to seek the union of your truth and God. They are one and the same. It is the Divinity inside you. It is not about loving yourself so much that you rise above everyone else. No! It is the opposite. It is about loving yourself so much that you are humble to all in the world. It is knowing that in serving you are served. It is a place of peace.

ANNA: How can we all better serve the world?

MARY: Follow the words of enlightened ones . . . be compassionate, eliminate prejudice, and love all people; open your hearts to love and receive love, embrace Divinity inside yourself, let people see how you live your life in connection with God, worship God and only God, pray not only for yourself but for others. If you do these things you will serve the world.

ANNA: Mother Teresa said, "If we have no peace, it is because we have forgotten that we belong to each other." Was Mother Teresa enlightened?

MARY: Mother Teresa did not seek enlightenment, yet she was enlightened. By her very nature she was a gift to humanity. Her words taught so many, her language spoke of compassion and being humble. She was pure in her quest to help others and break down barriers. She knew that the people of the world needed one another and that God connected all.

ANNA: Interesting . . . You say "Mother Teresa did not seek enlightenment, yet she was enlightened." So we don't actually have to seek it to reach it?

MARY: I am so pleased that you are hearing my every word! You don't have to seek enlightenment consciously in order to achieve it. If you live your life in accordance with the one true Love, which is God, you will reach that state. You will understand that living your life in this way is the path to all that you seek.

ANNA: Is there a special place in heaven for "enlightened" individuals?

MARY: There is no hierarchy in the kingdom except for God. All are of God's vibration. All are together in the kingdom. You may still learn from the energy of "enlightened" ones, but they can also learn from you. Know that the kingdom awaits you as well but you must allow it in and live with Love on earth. You still have much work to do on earth.

Meditation for Chapter Nine

✦ Gently close your eyes and breathe. Ask the angels
to surround you in a brilliant circle of light, love, and
protection. Imagine a column of light from heaven
moving into the crown of your head, spreading
through your body, and anchoring you to the core of
the earth. Feel this wonderful light moving through
your spinal column up from the tips of your toes.
Allow your body to relax as you focus on your breath.
Be aware of the rise and fall of your chest as you
breathe in all that is good and right in the universe. Be
aware that you are filling your lungs with the Divine
breath of God. Imagine your breath as a gentle wave
moving back and forth and back and forth. Feel your
body relax after each exhale as you release stress,
negativity, and all else that doesn't serve you. Be
conscious of how wonderful this feels. It is truly a gift
to permit relaxation and peace into your mind, body,
and soul.

✦ Allow the energy of Mary, of her love and peace, to
enter your body with each inhale. Exhale all that
doesn't serve you: all stress, anxiety, anger, animosity,
self-recrimination, and anything else that might get
in the way of connecting to heaven. As you move into
that wonderful place of total relaxation, begin to feel a
sensation of peace moving through your body. It feels
wonderful. Bask in this peace and relax. As you continue
to feel the rise and fall of your chest as you breathe,
imagine there is a silky pale blue light encircling your

body. You feel its gentle vibration as it swirls around
you, alerting and filling your senses. Just allow yourself
to be. Know that it is good. Let this vibration hug you
gently. Recognize this vibration as Mother Mary. Let
her warm presence move your focus from your breath to
the soft beating of your heart.

+ Envision your heart becoming larger in your chest as
you let her in. See the soft blue that is circling around
you ease into your physical body and your heart.
Imagine that your whole being is reaching out to her,
to be a part of her. As you allow the soft blue light to
fill your heart, recognize that both you and Mary are
blending energetically; you are becoming one essence.
Delight in knowing that you are vibrating with her
energy. As you breathe, begin to feel her more and more
and allow yourself to go deeper. Now imagine a clear
space, free of thought, and allow your breath to wander
in silence. Visualize Mary standing in front of you;
whatever image that works best for you is fine. She can
continue to be the pale blue light or a feeling, or perhaps
you may want to personify her. Again whatever feels
right.

+ Sense your connection to God. Imagine your soul
filled with goodness and compassion. Feel a strong
unconditional love surrounding you; it moves fluidly.
Allow it to enter your heart. This love is more abundant
and shines with a color that you have never seen before;
one that you can only feel and not see clearly. Feel a
sense of euphoria; it is beyond anything you have ever
experienced before. You are joyful and overwhelmed

with love. Know that this can only be God. Accept the peace that he brings as your body becomes a vessel for his love and his serenity. These are his blessings. You may not want to move for a bit. Sit in this Love, allow it to heal and enlighten you.

10

Finding Harmony
in Today's World

How Do We Manage the Day to Day?

ANNA: It seems like there are more and more people today either abandoning their religions or combining their religions with spirituality that incorporates Eastern as well as Western religions. For example, it may include yoga as a form of spirituality or shamanism, and so forth. What do you think of this?

MARY: If this movement toward spiritual collectiveness and unity incorporates compassion and strives for peace within the self and others, it is good. As long as the ultimate gratitude goes to God, it is good. People need to be cautioned about elevating the teacher. All people are the same; only God is above. Yet, if the teacher is not acting out ego and gratification of the self in spreading the Word of God, the teacher is blessed for bringing in the light.

ANNA: How can we, today, incorporate the Bible, the Quran, or any of the other holy books which were written thousands of years ago?

MARY: Seek not an intellectual interpretation of these books, but rather an understanding of the Love that speaks through the written words. In these texts, the message is love, peace, and compassion for all people. If these words, which are contained in other holy books, are followed, people will find inner peace and peace with each other. Also, the words and feeling of God is love, *not* discrimination, prejudice, righteousness, or domination. If the interpretation focuses on anger and destruction of people and nations, it does not come from the Creator of all people.

ANNA: How do we balance a modern God with the God described in the Bible, given that it was written over three thousand years ago. In other words, how do we decide what parts of the Bible to take literally and what to take figuratively?

MARY: My dear, this is a question that will take many discussions for a complete answer. In all of the holy books, there are many interpretations of the words written. The holy books were written by men, affected by their cultures and the time that they existed on earth. Keep in mind what was happening historically at the time these passages were written. Some of the standards of those days may not be relevant or fit in the present world. Over the centuries, cultures have changed, but the Word of God is as relevant today as it was when it was first written. Not all of the passages apply to people in your world, but the Bible contains truth. Also, there are many passages that are figurative to give examples on how to live in accordance with the will of God. Know that the parts to be taken literary speak of justice, truth, love, forgiveness, and peace. As you read, use your intelligence and heart to decipher the Truth. If you live following the love spoken of in these books, you will be doing right and God will be pleased. The holy books are not outdated; the world is still evolving and the books still hold the Truth of God.

ANNA: Many people today refer to God as "the power that is" or as "the universe." Is it okay to refer to God in this way?

MARY: My child, I have said God is not a person and he is the great "I Am." Again, people personify him because it makes it easier and makes logical sense for people to connect to a person than an invisible entity. Calling God the "power" or the "universe" is fine since he is both. God only cares that he is called! He wants all to come to him.

ANNA: Is there energy in our thoughts?

MARY: Yes . . . your thoughts have energy as does your physical being. Your thoughts affect the thoughts of people all over the world. You are a being of energy in every way. In this way, God made all perfectly! There are so many ways to share yourself with others.

ANNA: That's kind of cool when I think about it. Now I'm thinking on a global level! In recent decades Eastern medicine has burgeoned. Should we abandon the Newtonian medicine of the West and focus more on these Eastern practices, like Reiki where we are essentially working with God's energy?

MARY: There is a place for both conventional medicine and the flow of God's energy to help heal people. These practices will become more and more prevalent as more and more people use them. Someday, the two will work in tandem to heal at the highest level . . . healing the physical, the emotional, and the soul parts of people. The healing energy of God is around you and has always existed. God can and does heal through people. There are many stories of the many people healed by my son. The energy would leave his physical body to heal others. There is one story about a woman who traveled many miles to be with Jesus to receive a healing. She had been bleeding for twelve years and could not be healed. She touched Jesus's cloak in faith and was healed at once. Immediately Jesus realized that God's power had gone out from him. He turned around in the crowd and asked, "Who touched my clothes?" The woman, knowing what had happened to her, came and fell at his feet and, trembling with fear, told him the whole truth. He said to her, "Daughter, your faith has healed you. Go in peace and be freed from your suffering" (Mark 5:21–43, Matthew 9:18–26, Luke 8:40–56). Not only is this a story of faith, but it shows that my son felt the energy leave his body. Such is the case with those working with God's energy today. Each person has this energy. It is those who recognize it as the energy of God that can and will help many people. It is a function of love; the desire to help.

ANNA: So does this follow with the scripture that says, "As you go, proclaim this message: 'The kingdom of heaven has come near.' Heal the sick, raise the dead, cleanse those who have leprosy, drive out demons. Freely you have received; freely give" (Matthew 10:7–8)?

MARY: Yes, yes, yes! The proclamation is to act in pure faith as my son did. He is recognized as the greatest healer from those who are not only Christian but of all religions. Act in the way that he acted and heal each other! Remember, for those who are working with God's energy and loving vibration to bring healing, all gratitude and honor must go to God. Each person carries this healing energy but it is in connection with God that miracles can happen. And the phrase "the kingdom of heaven has come near" refers to the living, vibrating essence of Divinity and the kingdom of God in each and every person. When this energy is shared, healing and love is brought through for not only the person requesting to be healed but also the one bringing in the energy of God.

ANNA: Among the most popular energy medicine techniques used today is Reiki. Reiki claims to move innate Divine energy into the place where the person needs most to heal. Of course I understand that this energy may not always cure the person seeking healing. What do you think of that?

MARY: As long as the person who is doing the work acknowledges that they are a vessel through which the energy flows, it is right and good. All honor and glory for the healings go to God. And yes, when it is acknowledged that this energy has Divine intelligence, the energy moves to where the person needs it most, as determined by God. Reiki is wonderful and a return to many of the ancient ways of healing. Much of what you are seeing in the world today is a call to former ways of healing which were connected to God rather than science as a way to heal. Yet science has its place; there *is* a reason for its existence. As I said previously, the two must combine for people to really heal on all levels.

ANNA: There are so many stories about miracles in all of the holy books of various religions, yet we don't hear much about miracles occurring today. Are miracles just a thing of the past?

MARY: My daughter, what is a miracle? That is what you must ask yourself. Be aware of all that is around you. Open your eyes and you will see so many miracles! The intricacies of your bodies are illustration of what a miracle is. Waking up in the morning and seeing a beautiful sunlit sky is a miracle. Answered prayers, both large and small, are miracles. The birth of a child is a miracle. Awaken! Look at your lives and you will see small miracles every day. I understand that people seek the more spectacular miracles for validation; perhaps a mountain moving, or someone walking on water. Know that these miracles are still occurring and exist as surely as you exist; just because you have not seen them doesn't mean they haven't happened. If you recognize and accept the miracles already taking place in your own life and the lives of those around you, you will then see more miracles.

ANNA: I suppose it's simply a matter of perception and when we're busy we are blinded to so much of the beauty around us already. I am also thinking about the idea of peace. What is it, really? Is it lack of war?

MARY: Peace exists in communities and on a global level as well as within oneself. It is not just the absence of war among nations, but the absence of war within each person individually.

ANNA: How can we settle these "wars" within ourselves?

MARY: Pray and bring God into your lives. Peace comes to us in many ways. By recognizing and giving up much of what our ego desires, and refocusing on our soul and the spark of God within ourselves, we find peace. I know this is one of the most difficult things for people to do. As desires of a material nature are pushed aside, a sense of contentment will be felt internally, and peace will flow. Peace also comes to us when the mind is untroubled by misfortune, when our emotions are tranquil, and when we are free from fear and anger. Peace comes, too, when we relinquish attachments and are indifferent to success or failure. Peace flows when we know who we are, as a flesh and bone entity and as one of energy, light, and high vibration. Once you experience peace, you will know real joy.

ANNA: It sounds so beautiful, but to be truthful, I am not sure if it is attainable.

MARY: It is only unattainable if there is fear to give up what you "think" fulfills you. Material objects may bring you joy momentarily, but God brings permanent happiness. Finding peace doesn't mean one needs to live in poverty or reject the material things of the world, but rather to be satisfied with what one has.

There is nothing wrong with striving for more, yet it cannot be the primary reason for existence. The desire for more money and more things is a distraction from God and causes turmoil when it is a focus of life. Strive for more spiritually and make God your focal point.

ANNA: How can we separate ourselves from our misfortunes and our failures?

MARY: My dear one, you simply cannot and should not. It is by acknowledging these misfortunes and failures that you come to understand that they do not exist in a true sense but are simply consequences of your actions. You learn from them. The test is in how you react to things that don't go exactly as you desire. In perceiving failure as a learning experience and believing that God will provide another means of happiness, you begin to see how true faith works and what is necessary to find peace. If you are consumed by your successes and failures, you will never be able to find peace. Instead, you will be paralyzed with fear and anxiety. Yet, if you move through the currents of life, knowing that God is moving with you and showing you what will bring ultimate joy, you will be at peace. If you don't direct anger and self-recrimination at yourself and others, your soul will be calm and filled with peace. How wonderful is this internal peace! How wonderful it is to not feel the need to be better but recognize that you are good and right with God.

ANNA: So if we find this place of peace inside of ourselves, will it be contagious to other people?

MARY: If you are at peace, you will not react in negative ways to others. Instead, you will be filled with compassion for others. You will recognize that you have only love to gain from other people and nothing more. Nothing else matters. You will see people for who they really are. You will see the broken and may want to help them. You will also be able to identify those who are lighting the world and they will be attracted to you.

ANNA: You use the word *attract*. Do we attract certain people to us?

MARY: Yes, you do. Your energy seeks those who will teach you, help you find that peace inside yourself, guide you, and also help you to learn what you need to learn as you journey through life.

ANNA: And yet I feel that sometimes we attract people who may hurt us or fail to bring us joy?

MARY: Yes, sometimes you will attract those who provide an unpleasant relationship. And yet they will help you grow as a soul and as a person. Be thankful for the relationships in your life. They were meant to be, and ultimately, if you learn from them, the relationship will bring about peace.

ANNA: Can other people steal peace from those who have attained it?

MARY: My daughter, if your peace comes from the highest source, no one can steal it. You can share your peace and show others, by your actions and words, how to attain it for themselves. No one can give peace; it comes from deep within. My prayer is that all humanity finds this peace within themselves. Through this peace and acceptance of who they are, there will be no need to fight among one another.

ANNA: Can inner peace exist without global peace?

MARY: One leads to the other. If people find peace within themselves, this inspires acceptance of who they are as human beings and as souls. Once this is achieved even with one individual, that individual sheds judgment and antagonism toward other people which inspires similar behavior in others, eventually spreading to families, communities, and nations through-out the world.

ANNA: Various reports over the years have described statues of Mary weeping tears. What is the significance of this?

MARY: I weep for the world. I weep for the pain and suffering I witness. I weep for lack of peace and love and compassion among all people. I weep for you individually and collectively. My tears flow for those who cannot hear me and turn away from God.

ANNA: How can we help those who are not hearing your mes-sages?

MARY: Again, pray for the world and all its people; those who are filled with love and those who are filled with hatred and an evil need to destroy. Don't judge and condemn but pray for their salvation. These people know no love, peace, or even joy. Pray that their actions which hurt and destroy others will cease. Spread the word in small, peaceful ways so that the world can be saved not in war, but in an embrace.

ANNA: Can the world really be saved? Can wars end? Can we ever have peace?

MARY: I am here to tell you that if you focus on the goodness of the Lord and yourself; and see the connection between all people, it can be. The fight should be for harmony and peace, not power. People of the world need to speak up for this peace and love, and pray. There is so much that cannot be controlled, yet in prayer the diminishing of fear, anger, and power will manifest. I have said it before and will say it again, pray, pray, pray.

ANNA: To shift slightly, it is difficult for a parent to be at total peace. How do we not worry about our children? Mother, can you shed some light?

MARY: As parents you want to control your children in order to protect them in some way. Listen to me: You cannot control another person, just as God cannot control your actions. That is why I, the mother, am imploring you to heed my words. I cannot control you; I can simply lead you. You may do the same with your children. You can raise your children and teach them the ways of God. But you must surrender them to God for their well-being as people and souls.

ANNA: This reminds me of a passage in *The Prophet* by Kahlil Gibran, where he talks about our children not being our children, that they are sons and daughters of Life's longing; that they come through us but not from us and do not belong to us. Do you agree with this?

MARY: It is true and his words are perfect. If you can follow this, not only will you find peace, but so will your children and your children's children. It must be set in motion.

ANNA: What if we all find this peace that you speak about?

MARY: If you all find peace, then you will all find love. If this happens the gates of heaven will open and my job will be done. Ah, it is my greatest prayer. God wishes to share his light completely with you and all people together. It can be done.

ANNA: Mother, with all that you have shared with us . . . What can we do to save humanity and make this world a better place?

MARY: All my children must recognize that you all carry the very essence of Divinity and share the highest vibration. In that Divinity, you must speak and live the Truth of all that is.

ANNA: What is the Truth?

MARY: The Truth is recognizing that you are all beings of Love. The Truth includes sharing this commonality with each other.

You are not physical beings but rather beings of the light. You are souls. Don't be confused by illusion and fear. Frequently, you may see only what you want to see; let your eyes open to the unknown. Awaken, my children! See God as all that is good. Live the Truth of Love and the world will be born anew. Love leads to all that is good and right. It leads to God.

ANNA: But how can one person or a few people change the entire world?

MARY: As one person wakes up and begins to open their heart and speak the Truth from their heart, millions can be affected. This one person enlightens another, who speaks to another, and so on and so forth until a great fortress of peace and justice is built and all are thriving in Love. Open your hearts and let your hearts speak! Let your fear slip away and let your love for yourself and others expand. You will affect and touch multitudes of people.

ANNA: How can I better love myself?

MARY: You must cherish the mind, body, and soul that you have been blessed with. You must worship the Love inside of you and never let fear lead you astray. You are the embodiment of God and that in itself demands and commands love. Don't restrain your goodness, let it flow and reach the world. Be courageous and speak the Truth.

ANNA: What of the diseases in the world that so many people suffer from? Can our prayers really be answered?

MARY: Of course. You should pray for the end of all suffering. The world was created pure and without disease or sickness. Humanity has polluted and destroyed the environment. The air you breathe and the water you drink has become polluted and thus, created disease. You can pray and act in prayer. People must fight for laws to respect and keep the planet clean. Your grandchildren will suffer dearly if the planet is not purged of the poisons infecting the ground and the air. You must act in order to stop disease. Yet, always remember, humans live to one day pass through life and dwell in the kingdom. The gift of life is ultimately death and rebirth in the kingdom. Don't cry for those who pass on; rejoice for they are with God. They are at peace.

ANNA: Will you continue to pray for the world?

MARY: Until the very last second.

ANNA: Is that day coming soon?

MARY: Soon is relative . . . Pray for peace; pray for heaven on earth. It is not written when.

ANNA: So much of what you have said in our conversation goes back to connecting with you, God, and heaven through prayer. I understand that through prayer the world can change but prayer is a passive act.

MARY: Prayer is passive and active. It begins in your heart and soul, and promotes a connection to great Love that leads to an awakening of Truth and enlightenment. When one is awakened, fear is pushed aside and the prayer becomes active. People begin to be more compassionate and kind. They move from the quest for power to living in energy of the one who has always held the power. As I mentioned previously in our conversation, passive prayer leads to active prayer and your daily life becomes a prayer. Do you understand?

ANNA: I do understand. I will continue to pray . . . Mother, you have said that all praise and glory goes to God. I recognize God is the Almighty and the one who is deserving of praise. But I love you. Is it wrong to adore you?

MARY: My daughter, it is not wrong to adore me, but remember that God created me and all that is. God is most deserving and the one to whom all praise and honor should be directed . . . Love me, adore me as your mother who brings God, the supreme being, to you. I come to bring you the energy and vibration of God's love. Hear my words and praise God!

ANNA: I know that I will have so many more questions as my life continues. May I come to you and ask?

MARY: My daughter and all my children, as I have said, I am always here for you. I invite all people to come to me and talk to me and pray with me. I desire to be with all people and to pray with all people. Remember, no one is ever alone.

ANNA: With a sincere and overflowing heart I thank you for sharing your messages with me and the world. Mother, I know I speak for so many when I say, "I love you."

MARY: I know you speak for so many and for that I am grateful. I love all my children and I will continue to pray for and with all of you. I pray for your joy, peace, connection to the great Love, and for a world full of this Love and peace. It can be. I implore you to pray, pray, and pray, and walk hand in hand with the vibration of God. I want you to know that above all else, you are made from Love, exist with Love, and are the greatest Love. Amen.

Meditation for Chapter Ten

+ Gently close your eyes and breathe. Ask the angels to surround you in a brilliant circle of light, love, and protection. Imagine a column of light from heaven moving into the crown of your head, spreading through your body, and anchoring you to the core of the earth. Feel this wonderful light moving through your spinal column up from the tips of your toes. Allow your body to relax as you focus on your breath. Be aware of the rise and fall of your chest as you breathe in all that is good and right in the universe. Be aware that you are filling your lungs with the Divine breath of God. Imagine your breath as a gentle wave moving back and forth and back and forth. Feel your body relax after each exhale as you release stress, negativity, and all else that doesn't serve you. Be conscious of how wonderful this feels. It is truly a gift to permit relaxation and peace into your body, soul, and mind.

✦ Allow the energy of Mary, of her love and peace, to enter your body with each inhale. Exhale all that doesn't serve you: all stress, anxiety, anger, animosity, self-recrimination, and anything else that might get in the way of connecting to heaven. As you move into that wonderful place of total relaxation, begin to feel a sensation of peace moving through your body. It feels wonderful. Bask in this relaxation and peace. As you continue to feel the rise and fall of your chest as you breathe, imagine there is a silky pale blue light encircling your body. You feel its gentle vibration as it swirls around you, alerting and filling your senses. Just allow yourself to be, as this blue vibration floats around you. Know that it is good. Let this vibration hug you gently. Recognize this vibration to be Mother Mary. Let her warm presence move your focus from your breath to the soft beating of your heart.

♦ Envision your heart becoming larger in your chest as you let her in. See the soft blue that is circling around you ease into your physical body and your heart. Imagine that your whole being is reaching out to her to be a part of her. As you allow the soft blue light to fill your heart, recognize that both you and Mary are blending energetically; you are becoming one essence. Delight in knowing that you are vibrating with her energy. As you breathe, begin to feel her more and more and allow yourself to go deeper. Now imagine a clear space, free of thought, and allow your breath to wander in silence. Visualize Mary standing in front of you; whatever image that works best for you is fine. She can continue to be the pale blue light or a feeling, or perhaps you may want to personify her. Again whatever seems right or feels right.

♦ See yourself sitting in a circle on very green grass, under a bright orange sun with many people. Feel the warm healing rays of the sun caressing your head and neck. It feels so wonderful. You notice and recognize the blue energy of Mary coming toward you. Imagine Mary reaching out her hand to heaven and allowing God's healing to fill her. She then extends this energy to you and touches you on your body, allowing the energy to go where it is most needed; where God desires it to go. Feel this healing energy move through her into you; feel it flow through your body and your energy field, and settle as it goes. Feel the warmth of this energy and the serenity it brings to you. Imagine turning to the people on your right and reaching out to touch them on their heart. You feel Mary's energy, which continues to move through your body, move into your hands and into the heart of these people. See these people turn to the people on their right and touch them on their heart and so on until the healing energy flows freely around the circle. Sit in this energy, feel it, and be grateful for the healing. Recognize your connectedness with the others in the circle and notice the undeniable feeling of hope for the future. Thank God for his goodness as you continue to feel this energy flowing.

EPILOGUE

Mary belongs to all people. She is the mother of humanity and she is coming to break down barriers, not erect more division among people. Her words through this book speak to all people of every nationality and religious denomination. You may not agree with all that she says, but know that she speaks to mend a broken world and to bring the healing balm of love to all.

We must change our own views of the world and help bring Love to the forefront. I hope that Mary's words instill in you the motivation to find a way to help foster peace in the world by having compassion and love for yourself and your fellow human beings. If each one of us moves one foot in this direction, I am confident the world can and will change. One step at a time.

And so my prayer for you is that you listen to and feel the words that Mary has spoken through me in this book. I pray you feel her love as strongly as I did in writing down her answers. Maybe, that is my piece of heaven. I want so much to share that feeling with you and I truly believe that if you close your eyes and ask her to come into your heart, that if you let your heart feel, that if you tear down your own walls, you, too, can have your own conversation with the Mother Mary.

Pray, pray, pray.

HOT-BUTTON QUESTIONS
FOR A MODERN MARY

ANNA: Should priests get married if they want to?

MARY: The men who followed Jesus were married before and after his death.

ANNA: You discuss this in chapter five. Is there one "right" religion?

MARY: There are many paths that lead to heaven. There is no "right." As long as the religion promotes love and compassion to all creation, it is right.

ANNA: Is gay marriage a sin?

MARY: What is sin? Where there is love between two people it cannot be wrong.

ANNA: What are your thoughts on modern terrorism?

MARY: There have always been wars and atrocities. My thoughts on modern terrorism are no different than my thoughts on previous acts of war. The world needs to turn to God for this to end. Pray.

ANNA: What are your thoughts on racism, both in the United States and around the world?

MARY: We are all one in the eyes of the Creator. There is no place for any type of human oppression based on gender, race, religion, or nationality.

ANNA: What about gender inequality and the oppression of women on a global level?

MARY: My answer to this is similar to the one above. We are all one in the eyes of the Creator. Humans should not be afraid of change. Fear begets fear. Men *and* women need to see each other on equal footing in order for inequality and oppression to end.

ANNA: I know you touched on this in chapter seven but can you go into more detail on how you feel about prayer in school?

MARY: All glory to God in and out of school. Pray, pray, pray, and give glory to God wherever you are in a way that is best for you.

ANNA: How do you feel about the current refugee crisis?

MARY: It breaks my heart. Compassion must prevail.

ACKNOWLEDGMENTS

God has been so good to me on this journey. He has taught me directly, through my own experiences, and through the experiences of the souls of whom he has brought to me. They have been and will continue to be my diamonds; gems that money could never buy. I am so grateful to so many.

First and foremost, to my beloved Mary. It has been an honor to be her pen. This book is pure energy. It is filled with her love and her true voice. I hope you have been able to feel her energy as I do.

To my husband, Vinny, whose patience and support during the days it took to make this book come alive was the answer to an unsaid prayer. I am so grateful to have him as my partner in this life. To my sons, Matthew and Joseph, who are my greatest living teachers. They are truly wonderful, and their very existence helps me to understand the maternal love of Mary. Writing books aside, I am so grateful just to be their mom.

To my publisher and editor at Atria Books, Judith Curr and Johanna Castillo. I honestly believe that Mary, in her way, brought me to them, for she knew they would hear her. They recognized in some way that this book needed to come out and be in your hands. To Suzanne Donahue, Associate Publisher at Atria, who went out of her way to make sure that Mary's messages would be heard. They have been truly special partners in this endeavor and I am deeply grateful. Thanks to my editor, Wendy Ruth Walker, who painstakingly edited words and organized thoughts as I wrote without boundaries. And to Gibson Patterson, who helped me with social media, and Emi Battaglia, my wonderful public relations person. They, along with the terrific people at Atria, helped to bring me and this book into the public arena.

To Carrie DiRaffaele Silverstein, whose help during this project was beyond friendship. Not only did she help edit, but when I became overwhelmed with the words Mary was conveying, she pushed me forward.

To my parents, Patrick and Frances Acquafredda, who let me grow up knowing that what I was experiencing was real. So many times, parents discount the visions and intuition of their children and stop them from following their souls. My soul was able to flourish because my parents accepted my gift.

To my support group, the ladies whom I traveled to Medjugorje with, and my Rosary group: Monika Sywak, Tricia Riccardi, Iris Farmer, Carrie DiRaffaele Silverstein, Maria Teresa Ruiz, and Susan Reid. Your enthusiasm about this book was tangible and inspiring. To Nancy Pantoliano, Amy K. Russell, and Isabelle Bell, who have been my biggest cheerleaders since I began to do my spiritual work, and continue to be a constant source of positive energy. To my friend and hairstylist, Kathleen McEntire, who is always there with a brush and hairdryer to make me beautiful before each event. You are a magician! To Debora and Vincent Rosa for their hours of work on the graphics for my website as the book emerged. Deb and Vin put forward, in record time, what needed to be done. You all encourage me to keep writing, speaking, teaching, and sharing.

To each and every client that I have had the privilege of spending time with over the years: You have helped me expand my gift, and in turn, have taught me so much.

And to everyone else who has helped me on this journey. I feel truly blessed.

CONVERSATIONS
with
MARY

ANNA RAIMONDI

Reading Group Guide

On the following pages are some questions to pose during a book group meeting. Mary felt the following meditation might guide readers into discussion.

Meditation to
Open Your Heart and Mind

✦ Gently close your eyes and breathe. Ask the archangels
to surround you in a brilliant circle of light, love, and
protection. Imagine a column of light from heaven moving
into the crown of your head, spreading through your
body, and anchoring you to the core of the earth. Feel
this wonderful light moving through your spinal column
up from the tips of your toes. Allow your body to relax as
you focus on your breath. Be aware of the rise and fall of
your chest as you breathe in all that is good and right in
the universe. Be aware that you are filling your lungs with
the Divine breath of God. Imagine your breath as a gentle
wave moving back and forth and back and forth. Feel your
body relax after each exhale as you release stress, negativity,
and all else that doesn't serve you. Be conscious of how
wonderful this feels. It is truly a gift to permit relaxation
and peace into your mind, body, and soul.

✦ Allow the energy of Mary, of her love and peace, to
enter your body with each inhale. As you move into that
wonderful place of total relaxation, begin to feel a sensation
of peace moving through your body. It feels wonderful.
Bask in this relaxation and peace. As you continue to feel
the rise and fall of your chest as you breathe, imagine there
is a silky pale blue light encircling your body. You feel its
gentle vibration as it swirls around you, alerting and filling
your senses. Just allow yourself to be, as this blue vibration

floats around you. Know that it is good. Let this vibration hug you gently. Recognize this vibration to be Mother Mary. Let her warm presence move your focus from your breath to the soft beating of your heart.

+ Envision your heart becoming larger in your chest as you let her in. See the soft blue that is circling around you ease into your physical body and your heart. Imagine that your whole being is reaching out to her to be a part of her. As you allow the soft blue light to fill your heart, recognize that both you and Mary are blending energetically; you are becoming one essence. Delight in knowing that you are vibrating with her energy. As you breathe, begin to feel her more and more and allow yourself to go deeper. Now imagine a clear space, free of thought, and allow your breath to wander in silence. Visualize Mary standing in front of you; whatever image that works best for you is fine. She can continue to be the pale blue light or a feeling, or perhaps you may want to personify her. Again whatever seems right or feels right. Ask her to open your heart, mind, and soul to find the answers that are right and perfect for you.

BOOK CLUB DISCUSSION QUESTIONS

1. What information about Mary impacted you the most?

2. Mary speaks of raising the "vibration" of the world. What do you think she means by *vibration* and do you think this is possible?

3. Discuss the concept of the Ascended Master. Do you agree that someday all people will become Ascended?

4. How readily do you think Mother Mary can be accepted by all people when she has been viewed as the "Catholic Mother" for centuries?

5. Mother Mary talks about how she, the spirits, and angels have and continue to come through to help people. Have you ever experienced this?

6. Why do you think Mary says people are ready *now* to receive her message of peace?

7. What do you think Mary means when she says, "listen with your heart"?

8. Anna asks Mary whether healing can occur through prayer. Do you believe this? Have you experienced this?

9. Discuss Mary's statement: "There is no fate; only journeys." Do you believe in free will?

10. What do you think of the idea that humans are "souls with a covering"? The soul as a "compass"?

11. Mary talks about reincarnation. Have you ever felt that you have lived before in another lifetime?

12. There has been so much written about Mary, and there have been so many interpretations on who she was and is to us today. How do you think *Conversations with Mary* is different, in terms of her portrayal and message, than other books that exist?

13. How has this book affected you and your connection to other people and God? Has it changed your life in any way?

AUTHOR QUESTIONS AND ANSWERS

Q: When did you decide you were going to write this book?

A: You know, that is an interesting question. To be perfectly honest, the decision was kind of made for me. For the last twenty years or so, I have relinquished as much control over my life as possible. By doing so, things now just fall into my lap. I have learned that as God opens doors, I simply need to walk through. In this case, I met someone who introduced me to my editor at Atria Books. Johanna and I talked briefly about me writing a book. From the beginning we discussed the book being about Mary. I always had a book about Mary in the back of my mind and so it made sense to me. And so, with a brief synopsis of the book in hand, I met the folks at Simon & Schuster and Atria, was given a contract, and the labor of bringing this book to light began.

Q: Did you have a plan for this book?

A: Not really . . . I knew that the book would be Mary speaking; her messages. That is really the only plan I had. I didn't know where it would start or end. Whether she was waking me up in the middle of the night, interrupting my thoughts, or speaking as I sat at my computer, I let whatever she had to say come through. I didn't write this book . . . Mary did. With utmost care I typed as she dictated.

Q: Were you interested in everything she had to say to you?

A: Not all of it; some things I never really gave much thought to, such as evolution. That topic kind of took me by surprise. I was just the scribe.

Q: What is your process?

A: Before sitting down to write, I pray and meditate. I feel the presence of Mary and begin to write. She sometimes gives me the answers and I have to go back and write the questions. Sometimes, she gives me both.

Q: What does "her presence" feel like to you?

A: Mary's energy is soft yet strong, and overwhelms me. Often, my heart will begin to race and thoughts start flooding my mind. I hear her in my head in an organized and persistent way.

Q: Do you hear her in your own voice or in her voice?

A: Because she is in spirit and not an apparition who is standing in front of me and talking, her voice is more similar to my voice . . . It's more telepathic. I don't know how she speaks to others, but this is my experience with her.

Q: How do you know it is her?

A: For me, there is no denying it is her. I am a medium and have communicated with spirits my whole life. She comes through like a warm blanket. Her energy envelops me and almost numbs me. Other spirits don't have that effect on me. She makes me feel safe and comfortable as she speaks.

Q: How do you know it isn't the Evil One playing a trick on you?

A: First, as I said, I pray prior to communicating with her, and am therefore protected. Secondly, her words are to help, heal, and build us up. Evil wants to destroy. Evil always instills an uneasiness inside people. I am completely at ease and comfortable with her. I crave her words and become excited as I type. Sometimes my fingers can't keep up with her.

Q: Have you ever heard God?

A: We have all heard God. God comes through when we are completely silent. God is a feeling of pure, unconditional love. When I have felt God near me, I don't want it to ever go away. God speaks to me more in a feeling of pure unconditional love. The feeling is overwhelming and one that is full of compassion and very difficult to explain. This feeling overtakes and stills me to almost a numbness. It is a feeling of pure exhilaration and bliss. I know without question that when I feel this it is God. I can only say it is a different sensation than the way I feel when Mary speaks to me. With Mary I get a sense that is loving but also more conversational. I hope that makes sense; it's difficult to describe.

Q: How can we hear Mary?

A: Talk to her, ask her to come to you in whatever way is best for you. Ask her to pray with you. Feel her energy around you.

Q: Now that the book is finished, will you continue to communicate with her?

A: Of course. I hope to all my life.

Q: What do you hope will happen as a result of this book?

A: I hope and pray that people will read her words and hear all that she has to say. She repeats over and over to pray and to love each other. It seems so simple . . . maybe it is.

Q: Do you pray to Mary?

A: As she says, she prays *with* us as we pray to God. God is the one who answers prayers. Mary is a strong intercessor of our prayers.

Q: Why do we need an intercessor? Why can't we just pray directly to God?

A: You can. She says that she delights in praying with us and can comfort us as we pray.

Q: Is this the end for you? What will you do now with the communication you receive?

A: If I could I would shout these messages from the highest mountain! At this point, I will follow where she leads me. As God opens up the doors, I will walk through them and let the world know all that I hear so perhaps there can be peace someday soon. Isn't that what we all want? Peace and love . . . as it was in the beginning, let it be now, as it will be, into eternity.